THE MOST AVOIDED QUESTIONS

A philosophical morality challenge

Jim Reay

www.jimreaywriter.net

First published in Queensland, Australia 2017

Copyright © James E Reay

The moral right of the author has been asserted.

All rights reserved.

No part of this publication may be reproduced, stored in a retrieval system or transmitted in any form or by any means without the prior permission of the publisher, nor be otherwise circulated in any form of binding or cover other than that in which it is published.

There are referenced quotes in this book, given as evidence for statements or arguments made. It is the author's understanding that such referencing falls within the educational and fair use provisions of copyright acts. Should anyone have concerns with the use, they are invited to contact the author at jr71@outlook.com.au

National Library of Australia Cataloguing-in-Publication entry:

Creator: Reay, Jim E., author.

Title: The most avoided questions : a philosophical morality challenge / Jim Reay.

ISBN: 9780994377845 (paperback)

Subjects: Ethics.

    Values.

    Many-valued logic.

Edited by Patrice Shaw www.psediting.com.au

Page layout and cover design by Kirsty Ogden www.epiphany.editing.com.au

Available worldwide on Amazon books.

eBook (ISBN: 9780994377852) available on Kindle, Kobo, Nook/Barnes & Noble and Apple.

Acknowledgements

My previous writings have been in the world of fiction – for me, an easier way to allude to the truth while sharing mystery stories. This is my first venture into the world of non-fiction.

The irony is that I have been provoked into it by seeing so much fiction out there in the real world which is either being misrepresented as fact or is part of fallacious attempts to influence and control thinking.

If the writing has worked for you, it is in no small way due to the fine editing of Patrice Shaw (www.psediting.com.au). Patrice brings a wisdom and a perceptive critical mind to the way in which words are used. She has given me significant help in my development as a writer.

Credit for the cover design and page layout should be given to Kristy Ogden (www.epiphanyediting.com.au). Kirsty has a graphic designer's eye for colour tones, balance and striking effects while bringing her editing skills to laying out the final package. She also has years of experience with the nuances of the publishing industry.

I am happy to recommend Patrice and Kirsty to anyone who wants to work with a frank, trusting team to get their stories out into print.

Thanks to my brother, Lewis. He has read all my developing manuscripts with his eye for detail and for continuity. His encouragement is greatly appreciated.

Thanks also to my wife, Brenda, and to our extended family for giving me the space and support to write.

There are others who have helped to form the ideas in this book while with me on long walks or chats over coffee or a beer. You are all appreciated.

Finally, please accept my gratitude to you, my regular or new readers, for giving your time to give value to my writing.

No man is an island
John Donne (1572–1631)

Other books by Jim Reay

Check on the author's website to read sample chapters of the books below:

www.jimreaywriter.net

Novels

Soft cover available on Amazon. (Search on Amazon.com. Books. Jim Reay.)

eBooks are available on Kindle, Kobo, Nook/Barnes & Noble and Apple.

The Napoleon Curse	ISBN	9780994377821
eBook	ISBN	9780994377838
Roller Coaster	ISBN	9781875872930
eBook	ISBN	9780994377883
The Run	ISBN	9781875872916
eBook	ISBN	9780994377876
Searching for Siobhan	ISBN	9781875872893
eBook	ISBN	9780994377869
The Chess Board	ISBN	9780994377807
eBook	ISBN	9780994377814

Young Adult

Catching Legends	ISBN	9781875872886

(Available only from Rams Skull Press, Brassall, Queensland, Australia https://www.ramsskullpress.com)

Short Stories

(Available on www.jimreaywriter.net)

'Humble'

'Losing it'

'Bush Wisdom'

'Lineage'

'The Child and the Bondi Islets'

Dare quam accipere
To give rather than to receive

In memory of those profound individuals of integrity and vision, who were positive and challenging role models for their succeeding generations.

Introduction

Morality is about the sense of something being right or not right.[1] How do we decide?

This book will examine the historical and scientific evidence as to how we regularly make moral decisions about difficult issues. We will draw upon the thinking of traditional Western philosophers. But we will also embrace the philosophical principles from the traditions of Africa and Asia; and, in particular, the Middle East. At the end of the process, we want to able to answer the question made famous by physicist, Julius Sumner Miller.[2]

'Why is it so?'

The litmus tests for morality should be based on a level of thinking that passes the scrutiny of logical reasoning and is testable. That will challenge any moral solutions which are based on tradition or dogma or 'alternative truths'[3], unless they can also meet the standards of good critical process.

We shall examine a range of topics – some immersed in cultural practice and some historical – that exist because that is the way it has always been done.

The paragraphs will generally be short and the chapters (below) should each induce questioning by critical minds.

1. Is telling the truth an important principle?
2. Should people have a right to say what they think – to express an opinion?

THE MOST AVOIDED QUESTIONS

3. Who decided that all human life is sacred and must be protected? Does that apply to ALL life?
4. Is 'human nature' programmed into our DNA or is it instilled by our cultural training?
5. Are parents responsible for their children?
6. Do only some belief systems have the answers for the future? Whether or not that is correct, why is it important?
7. Were the Dark Ages really dark?
8. Is it right to accumulate as much wealth as you can?
9. Can philanthropy and self-regulation solve the world wealth imbalance?
10. Economic growth is the only way forward, even at the expense of using up natural resources. Is that right?
11. Is it human nature to put people into 'boxes', categories – he/she is 'that type of person'?
12. Does context affect human rights?
13. Fallacies or fact. Are media factoids being believed?
14. Is the definition of morality the prerogative of the self-righteous? Are some people naturally superior and others inferior?
15. Is survival of the species more important than human rights?
16. Are we all brainwashed and the notion of free will is a myth?
17. Democracy is a term used to describe a country run by the people, of the people and for the people. Is that what it really is?
18. Are other alternatives to democracy clearly bad?
19. Whose rules are right in a global society? For example, refugees – humanity or someone else's problem?
20. Should the next generation have life better than we have had?
21. The conclusion – Now, how do you think moral decisions are made? The way forward? … and when?

I am not a professor of philosophy.

I am a humble asker of questions with a critical-thinking mind and a need to check information.

My hope is that, together, we can get closer to understanding the basis for some tricky moral dilemmas. The challenge for you, the reader, is to examine your assumptions or to imagine other beliefs.

My working hypothesis is that every moral decision is a prisoner of its time and culture.

But sometimes, the moral decisions are frozen in the unchallengeable dogma of belief systems, or they become entrenched in laws of the land or they are accepted as inalienable truths enforced by international agreements, declarations, conventions or constitutions.

The following chapters will address the theories above and test them against the logic of their historical roots – and that is just the start.

Author's Note

- Each chapter has its own references – many as links to the Internet – and they are accumulated in chapters after the text, as end notes.
- The references are supplied as the sources for the statements given, rather than undoubted, factual determinations. (In eBook versions, the reference hyperlinks are active.)
- I do not claim a complete coverage of viewpoints although I trust that there is sufficient balance for you to test 'the most avoided questions' against history and logic.
- The certainty of doubt is an underlying premise for all the discussions in this book … as it is in scientific inquiry. Readers are encouraged to conduct their own research where matters might be contentious.
- Dates are shown as BCE – *Before Current Era* or CE – *Current Era*, where any numerical confusion might occur.
- For the purposes of this book, morality is taken to mean how the individual might differentiate between right and

wrong. Ethics are taken to be the wider moral principles of social regulatory responses to difficult questions.

There are many paths to the top of a mountain but the view is always the same.

Chinese proverb

Chapter 1

Is telling the truth an important principle?

Aren't we trained from an early age to always tell the truth? It is part of our growing up – from toddler to child to adolescent to adult. But is that what we do?

Plato (circa 428–348 BCE)[4], the Greek philosopher and student of Socrates[5], would disagree with the parental advice, in part. He considered that there were two main groups of lies.

First, there are those lies that you would tell to enemies to protect your friends … as well as those that you would tell to the young to imbue them with a sense of respect. These are the good lies.

Plato approved of telling a good lie when giving the whole truth would be the wrong thing to do – where your weaknesses might become known to enemies, thereby allowing your people to be defeated. Socrates, the acknowledged founder of Greek philosophy, and Cephalus, a wealthy Greek elder, agreed with him.[6] *You look after your own* was their message.

Is that a fair moral position?

Plato believed that the young should be told stories about truth and honesty to instil in them a proper moral standard. In his view, these are some more of the good lies. He considered that children should only be told good moral stories because their minds have not developed sufficiently to understand the deeper meaning of allegories.

The bad lies, in Plato's terms, are those which are calculated breaches of trust, intended to deceive in a dishonourable way rather than in a caring or jocular fashion ... especially when another lie has to be told to cover the first.

Trust is important in many aspects of society.

For example, in a court of law, the judge is trying to get to the facts around a potential breaking of the law. Clearly, it is a benefit to know that he/she is hearing the truth.

Our law courts require us to swear oaths or to take affirmations that we will tell the truth, the whole truth and nothing but the truth. There are penalties of perjury for those who then choose to tell lies.[7]

The 2016 election campaign in the United States of America had clear, often bizarre, falsehoods being thrown out to the listening public, many of whom picked up the mantras and chanted the falsehoods back. It whipped up a crowd hysteria.[8]

And yet, this was an election for one of the most powerful positions in the world. *Was that the right thing to do?*

Should we accept that flamboyant language, which may also be erroneous, is alright from potential leaders when seeking election in democracies?

A similar frenzy occurred in Britain with the Brexit vote, about whether or not the United Kingdom should leave the European Union, also in 2016.[9] Fact checkers found many errors or deliberate falsehoods in the US and UK ballots, as well as the Australian federal election campaign of that year. (See the links)[10]

Does it matter that the claims were intended to deceive in order to gain a favourable result in the power play for election?

A factoid is a modern term for an invented piece of false information which appears in print and is repeated so often that people accept that it must be accurate.[11] The technique has been a mainstay of propagandists for decades and it is, effectively, telling lies.

Josef Goebbels[12], the Nazi propaganda minister in mid-20th century Germany, developed such misinformation into a refined art, with the result that his political party gained power and caused many citizens to question their understanding of right and wrong.[13]

Yet, the American constitution has the First Amendment which protects the right of citizens to say what they like, even if it is not true – with very few limitations, such as slander.[14]

So, is that the same as a little 'white lie' to spare someone's feelings?

An article[15] from American author, Frank Sonnenberg, suggests that people need to be able to trust one another, as a general principle. If someone develops a reputation for being a liar, then the trust is shattered and the person will forever be treated with suspicion.

On the other hand, there are many situations when gentle misrepresentations of the truth might be tactful. For example, if a student is developing skills, you might choose to acknowledge small improvements to encourage the person to keep trying – rather than being brutal and saying, *'Your best is not good enough'* or *'That is not even close to the expected standard'*.

While the gentle encouragement is not the real or whole truth, is it different from stating outright lies? Some might say that it is different because the encouragement is intended to be benign; a kindness.

An outright lie, by contrast, is a direct intent to deceive. It might be a straight denial *'I didn't do it'* or a total misrepresentation such as

'That person is a witch' or *'This car will drive for the next ten years and need no fuel'.*

We are now dealing with questions of social interaction.

As suggested in the Introduction, the context will probably play a part. But 'telling the truth' is also a matter of personal integrity and respect for others. The Chinese philosophers call such connections 'Hé', or Harmony[16] and much of their thinking is based on general relationships, rather than the particular.

George Washington, the first president of the United States of America was reputedly asked *'Who cut the cherry tree?'* and he reputedly replied, *'I cannot tell a lie. I chopped the cherry tree with my hatchet.'*[17] He has since been lauded throughout history as an example of the proper moral standard of honesty.

Was the story a lie? Or was it just a story to help children understand the value of honesty? There is an irony there.

The questions we might ask now could include:

Is there a right time to tell the truth and at other times it can be varied a little?

Whatever answer you give is a moral statement of your values and perhaps the culture that you grew up in – or your flexibility to resist following a mandated route.

Joseph Fletcher, in *Situation Ethics*[18] suggests that there are three approaches to making decisions, including moral decisions:

- Legalism – where the decision is made entirely in the context of a society's established codes and rules.
- Antinomianism – which is the polar opposite of legalism. In this mode, a decision follows no rules. It is spontaneous, even random. Precedent counts for nothing.
- Situationalism – which is between the other two. Here, the decision maker is fully armed with the ethical maxims of

his community or heritage and he/she uses them to illuminate the situation which presents itself.

Fletcher argues that, for the situationalist, 'telling the truth' is at most a maxim (an understanding of proper behaviour), not a rule. He uses the notion of love to explain that: *'The situationalist holds that whatever is the most loving thing in the situation is the right and good thing.'*

That is not dissimilar from St Augustine's (354–430 CE) principle of, *'Never use the truth to injure'* [19] or Plato's view on good and bad lies.

Should we expect people in positions of social authority to always tell the truth?

For some people, being told deliberate lies by public officials when they are expecting to be told the truth is an unpardonable breach of trust. The truth is the moral standard that they expect. Being lied to is injurious to them.

Other people appear to be able to tolerate some lies, as long as the core promises are not breached, because they have learned to expect some rhetorical flair (witty distractions, exaggerations or false promises) to happen from time to time, especially on political campaign trails.

Do you expect public officials to exaggerate or to make false promises?

Why have you learned that expectation? Do you have a moral line regarding how the truth should be told by people in social authority?

Are there times when you must tell the truth even if it hurts someone else?

While some people would accept St Augustine's maxim of never using the truth to injure, many societies have imposed legal guidelines which can do just that, for particular cases. For example, we have already mentioned courts of law who can invoke perjury penalties for anyone giving false evidence.

In Australia, royal commissions have powers to compel witnesses to give truthful evidence whether or not that might have negative implications for others.[20] They can then refer any breaches to the public prosecutors for court action and punishment.[21]

Australian parliaments have penalties for any government minister, member or senator who deliberately misleads the parliament by telling falsehoods. They could be expected to resign and/or even face criminal charges.[22]

And yet, similar behaviour outside the parliament is often tolerated as acceptable political spin.[23]

Why is that tolerated?

Is it to do with perceptions about freedom of speech … that people should be entitled to say what they want and how they choose to say it? (See Chapter 2).

Knowledge is like the baobab tree.
No one person can embrace it with both arms.

African proverb

Chapter 2

Should people have a right to say what they think – to express an opinion?

'Freedom of speech' has been the mantra of democratic societies, at least since the period of The Enlightenment (17th–19th centuries CE).[24]

The First Amendment of the United States constitution enshrines the principle of freedom of religion, freedom of speech or expression, including the press, and freedom of peaceful assembly.[25]

> *Amendment 1. Congress shall make no law respecting an establishment of religion, or prohibiting the free exercise thereof; or abridging the freedom of speech, or of the press; or the right of the people peaceably to assemble, and to petition the government for a redress of grievances.*

The United Nations Universal Declaration of Human Rights, Article 19, from 1948, states:

> *Everyone has the right to freedom of opinion and expression; this right includes freedom to hold opinions without interference and to seek, receive and impart information and ideas through any media and regardless of frontiers.*[26]

Voltaire, the 18th century French philosopher,[27] is often quoted as saying:

'I disapprove of what you say, but I will defend to the death your right to say it.'

It is a strong defence of the right to freedom of speech. Although it is more likely that those actual words were written by Evelyn Beatrice Hall[28] who was paraphrasing Voltaire's meaning.[29]

In January 2015, two gunmen entered the offices of *Charlie Hebdo* in Paris and killed twelve people, as well as injuring eleven others. *Charlie Hebdo* is a weekly satirical newspaper which produces cartoons that are intended to provoke and poke fun into sensitive areas – particularly at religious organisations, most recently the Muslim faith. Indeed, in 2013, the main cartoonist and editor-in-chief, stated: *'We have to carry on until Islam has been rendered as banal as Catholicism.'*[30]

On one hand, the murders in 2015 were clearly heinous crimes against the laws of France. On the other hand, *Charlie Hebdo* had been warned about such a reaction for years before … and they continued under the mantra of freedom of speech/expression.

In 2006, Islamic organisations took *Charlie Hebdo* to the French court using laws against hate speech to challenge their printing of cartoons that, in their view, were offensive, blasphemous and incited hatred towards Muslims.[31] However, the laws against blasphemy were revoked in 1791 in all parts of France, except in Alsace and Moselle.[32] The court action failed when the ruling stated that the cartoons targeted fundamentalists (a minority with extreme interpretations of traditional texts), not Islam itself.[33]

In France, the law on Freedom of the Press was passed on 29 July 1881[34] with several prohibitions such as Article 24 which:

> *prohibits anyone from publicly inciting another to discriminate against, or to hate or to harm, a person or a group for belonging or not belonging, in fact or in fancy, to an ethnicity, a nation, a race, a religion, a sex, or a sexual orientation, or for having a handicap.*

The penalty for violating this prohibition is up to a year of imprisonment and a fine of up to €45,000, or either one of those, as well as the suspension of some civil rights in some cases. The penalty for insult is up to six months of imprisonment and a fine of up to €22,500, or either one of those punishments.

So, clearly, in France, the laws are intended to curtail the freedom to say whatever a person chooses if it is likely to discriminate, defame or insult people in a particular religion. Yet, *Charlie Hebdo* persisted with more provocative cartoons in 2009, 2011, 2012 and 2014. This was despite numerous calls for them to desist by certain fundamentalist Muslims and despite several foiled attempts on the lives of the cartoonists over the years.[35]

After the massacre, a worldwide social and conventional media surge of support called on everyone to be *Je suis Charlie*, to protest against the atrocity.[36] Millions were carried along by the mantra and the understandable shock of the murders.

On the other side of the argument, the homogeneity of the media reporting left little space for many to question whether or not total freedom to write or draw defamatory images was indeed the intent of free speech. There was minimal coverage given to any who might say, *Je suis **non** Charlie* – to stand and argue against the French newspaper's strategy to mock particular religions.

There is little doubt that sections claiming to follow the Muslim faith had expressed their opposition over several years because they believed that the cartoons were defaming their Holy Prophet, Muhammad[37] and that under their interpretation of Sharia law[38], that was not only unacceptable but punishable by death.

So, here we have two contrasting legal and cultural views on the same incident.

What is the correct moral position?

Charlie Hebdo might argue that they have every right, under French law, to mock a religion which they choose to see as archaic. In an intellectual sense, they can hold whatever view they choose.

On the other hand, when freedom of speech is used to insult or humiliate people who are different or have a different view of the world, it raises the moral question of whether the powerful or 'the free' should be able to use that power against the less powerful or the less free.

Should people who follow a fundamentalist version of the faith be protected from other people who wish to exert their power of freedom of speech to say what they choose – even if that freedom of words or actions causes grief to those on the receiving end?

Should people who have a fundamentalist belief in their righteousness be able to incite followers to violence as retribution?
Right or wrong, clearly that can happen and has happened ... and it is not peculiar to one religion. The Catholic Church carried out inquisitions against suspected heretics and witches from the 13th to the 19th centuries, with extreme torture and death being used, particularly in the 15th to 18th centuries.[39]

But is it right?
It seems to depend on the perspective and time. We shall return to this in later chapters.

Australia has held a similar debate over clause 18c in the Australian Racial Discrimination Act.[40] 18c states:

> *(1) It is unlawful for a person to do an act, otherwise than in private, if:*
>
> *(a) the act is reasonably likely, in all the circumstances, to offend, insult, humiliate or intimidate another person or a group of people; and*
>
> *(b) the act is done because of the race, colour or national or ethnic origin of the other person or of some or all of the people in the group.*

Section 18d qualifies that section by stating that a prima facie breach of 18c will not be unlawful if it is done 'reasonably and in good faith' for artistic, academic, scientific or other public interest purposes (or in reporting on any such conduct).

Those people opposed to 18c's existence present several arguments:
- One is whether words can actually offend, humiliate and intimidate.
- A second argument is more legal in context. In all other aspects of Australian jurisprudence, a breach of law is based on what a reasonable member of the community would accept. However, with 18c, the breach can be judged by the recipient of the comment, not the reasonable community in general. That, the opposers argue, is inconsistent with the rest of Australian law.[41]

On the other hand, those who wish 18c to remain argue that it is the powerless people of society who have been vilified for decades and centuries. They are the ones needing protection from the words of the powerful.

That is a particular moral stance.

Furthermore, if the legal test is what a reasonable member of the community would expect, then minorities could argue that a random group of reasonable Australians would be unlikely to be representative of racial, sexual or handicapped minorities – those against whom demeaning language has often been directed.

The historical context of modern Australia is that the continent was colonised in 1788 by Britain, under the guise that the land was unoccupied, *terra nullius*.[42] That erroneous legal notion was overturned by the Mabo decision in 1992.[43] But in the two hundred years before, Aboriginal people had been subjected to massacres,[44] been forcibly removed to mission settlements and used as slave or low paid workers,[45] been denied the right to vote or even having their existence acknowledged in the censuses, had their children taken away from parents and removed to missions or foster homes,[46] been routinely denigrated in jokes and denied normal service in the community's shops as well as the opportunities that white people were given.

Given that background, do the persecuted deserve the protection that 18c could provide, albeit moderated by 18d?
Should powerful people be able to make disparaging comments, whether or not they are true? Is that just reinforcing negative stereotypes in the minds of the powerful and others?

Perhaps most would argue that offensive lies should never be allowed in the public domain. (See St Augustine's quote in Chapter 1). Interestingly, for over a hundred years in Australia and England, common law – specifically the law of torts – has had provision against defamatory comments.

However, to put it in a social context, an Irish judge, Sir James Matthews (1830–1908) reputedly said of the English legal system, *'In England, justice is open to all – just like the Ritz Hotel'*.[47] Maurice Hayes points out the humorous, logical fallacy in that statement – an oxymoron.[48]

Perhaps it is that the provision of the law of torts is less well known to the general public in Australia or that it was only really available to those who had the resources to take the matters through the courts.[49] By contrast, 18c of the Australian Racial Discrimination Act has a higher profile, particularly after several well publicised, real and potential court cases. The general public is probably more aware that racial taunts, or indeed false claims of the same, are not acceptable under that law.

In a moral sense, can there be a right and wrong answer to provoking others who think differently?
The 'rightness' of your view may well depend on your context/situation, your opportunities for a broad critical education, your freedom

to express your own opinion safely, your experiences in the power plays of society and your familial beliefs.

In a similar vein, in 2015, Pope Francis – head of the Catholic Church – defended freedom of speech but said that there were limits. The pontiff said that religions had to be treated with respect, so that people's faiths were not insulted or ridiculed. Using an analogy to illustrate his point, he told journalists that if his assistant cursed the Pope's mother, he could expect a punch from the pontiff.[50] Apparently, it is not just one religion that would react violently, if offended.

Should the courts have a role in determining whether or not commentary with elements of a factual basis might have crossed a line between unbiased reporting or taking the opportunity to ingrain prejudice?

Currently, under 18c or the law of torts in Australia, it is the case that courts can make such determinations. This chapter flags that most democratic societies have laws to regulate what sorts of speech are acceptable, often to protect the vulnerable, and that the law courts are charged with the responsibility to make such judgements, within their own countries.

However, there is a bigger picture.

When derogatory views come into conflict with the laws and beliefs of **other** countries, there can be international (cross-border) consequences and a judgement needs to be made at what point such confrontation is necessary or acceptable; for example, as in protest movements or expressing dissent.

'Right' and 'wrong' are perhaps not sufficiently refined definitions for the subtleties and responsibilities of when and how to intervene in the affairs of other countries.

Diplomacy is an example of a restrained form of speech and negotiation, designed not to offend other countries but to find acceptable solutions to problems. It generally deals with international conflicts and opposing views on the world. Diplomacy, however, can also be criticised for appearing to be a policy of appeasement – avoiding taking real action to address the hard moral decisions.

For example, in the context of the catalogue of alleged atrocities against its own people by the Syrian regime in recent years,[51] is there a difference between a spontaneous retaliation in moral outrage (such as the US missile attack on a Syrian airfield in April 2017) as compared to a steady calculated imposition of sanctions and a mustering of diplomatic pressure (as used by the previous US administration)? Is the second more an example of appeasement? Or are they both just attempts to appease consciences rather than to end the abuse?

Your upbringing might well give you a sense of certainty to state what you believe to be a correct moral response.

Is that, in itself, sufficient logic to intervene in the sovereign rights of other countries, who hold different views on morality?

If so, at what point should intervention occur? And to achieve what outcome?

Another example of **the policy of appeasement** was exemplified by British prime minister, Neville Chamberlain, with Nazi Germany's leader, Adolf Hitler, in 1938. It is often quoted as being a wrong approach because Chamberlain ignored the known discriminatory crimes against parts of the community being practised in German-occupied territories at the time and that Hitler was effectively lying.[52] World War II followed shortly afterwards – but it would likely have been the result anyway. There were larger global agenda at work.

In Chamberlain's defence, he would have been making a pragmatic decision. It would have been a huge responsibility to commit his country to war, particularly since Britain was clearly unprepared for such a conflict after World War I and the Great Depression. In the meantime, it was well known that Germany had been militarising throughout the later 1930s. In the event, the situation overtook the diplomatic manoeuvring.

A freedom of speech which has too many constraints could be the opposite of that free expression.

Freedom of expression is a structural safeguard built into the separation of powers and into most democratic constitutions. That safeguarding process can enable the general public to question how they are governed, to hold the elected representatives to account and to understand issues better. It also gives the general public the right to protest peacefully, without the threat of being locked up, beaten up or worse.

In non-democratic societies, freedom of speech is frequently denied and dissent is suppressed because their leaders do not wish to be questioned. In several countries, protest certainly can mean arrest, torture and even capital punishment.[53] Dictators, some hereditary royals or sham-elected presidents want the right to rule in the manner that they choose.

In democracies, the degree of control over free speech or demonstrations is a fine balance. Judgements, therefore, need to be made to establish at what point speaking out is the preferred or accepted option in contrast to remaining restrained or diplomatic. Often the decision is made by law enforcement on the grounds of maintaining public order … but there needs to be many transparent checks and balances when high emotions are involved.

The history of people provoking reactions from the alienated would suggest that a harmonious society would be better served by what, in earlier times, would be called good manners and respect for others – a discreet form of free speech.

THE MOST AVOIDED QUESTIONS

*If you don't know where you are going,
any road will take you there.*
Lewis Carroll

Chapter 3

Who decided that all human life is sacred and must be protected?

Does that apply to ALL life?

One of the earliest documented sources of the concept, 'Thou shalt not kill', comes from the Old Testament of the Bible and it is in the Jewish Torah.[54] It is given as a moral imperative in the Ten Commandments delivered by Moses. From that Judeo-Christian source appears to flow the current notion that 'all life is sacred'.[55]

> *The sanctity of human life has become an important tie between the ethics of religion and the ethics of the law in western democracies, and in many other lands.*

The terms *murder*, *homicide* and *manslaughter* would be familiar to most readers, as terms in the criminal codes of nations.

One of the oldest written legal statements against the crime of murder, written between 2100 and 2050 BCE, is in the code of Ur-Nammu, then located around the Tigris and Euphrates rivers in present-day Iraq. The code states, *'If a man commits a murder, that man must be killed'.*[56]

In Islam, according to the Qu'ran, one of the greatest sins is to kill a human being who has committed no fault (Qu'ran 5–32).[57]

And yet, throughout documented history, man has killed often with impunity in countless invasions and changes of ruler or regime. Many countries and cultures still have capital punishment as the final penalty for breaking social rules.

The *Hashashin*, from which the term assassin is derived, thrived from the 8th to the 15th centuries CE throughout the Middle East.[58]

Thuggees in India are reputed to have killed one million people between 1740 and 1840 CE.[59]

The Central American Aztecs of 14th to 16th centuries CE, among many cultures, believed that human sacrifice to the gods was essential for the continuation of their culture and, according to their codices recorded by Spanish conquerors, they killed many hundreds every year in regular monthly ceremonies of god appeasement.[60]

So, what happened to the *sanctity of life* and *thou shalt not kill*?
Even in the Bible, a distinction is drawn between *unlawful killing* – reflected in the laws of the times – which is different from *lawful killing* such as in the context of warfare, capital punishment or self defence.[61]

In some cultures, **honour killing** is accepted – where the family will kill a female member who has shamed the family in the eyes of their society.[62] In 2000 CE, the United Nations estimated that 5,000 women died in honour killings, each year, across the world.[63] This is most common in cultures where men rule their societies by fear and repression, using particular interpretations of customs which suit men's power, and with women only really being valued for their fertility function.[64] In many countries, including Western ones, the legal system does not address honour killing as being distinct from other domestic violence, because of cultural sensitivities.[65]

A Philosophical Morality Challenge

Whose morality is right?

In other cultures, the notion of **payback** has been an accepted means of redressing a death by murder.[66] That could mean that an innocent person from another tribe or family would be killed as payback or retribution.

That also happens in modern society. It could be argued that coalition invasions into Afghanistan and Iraq were a form of payback for the attack on the Twin Towers in New York on 9/11/2001.[67]

For many years, **genocide** was accepted as the consequence of an army losing in war or being the weaker ethnic group in conflicts over land. Throughout history, deaths from this type of killing of human life have run into many millions, in all parts of the world.[68]

However, since 1948 and the development of the United Nations Convention on the Prevention and Punishment of the Crime of Genocide, there have been significant legal cases which have helped clarify the international rationale and consequences for those who would commit or endorse genocide.[69]

Article 1 states:

> *The Contracting Parties confirm that genocide, whether committed in time of peace or in time of war, is a crime under international law which they undertake to prevent and punish.*

With this statement, '**in peace or war**', there is no international immunity irrespective of past accepted practice.

So, in the 21st century, we have laws that are generally accepted and which criminalise murder – the deliberate taking of human life without legal reason.

Doctors take the Hippocratic Oath[70] that they will do everything in their power to save life or, at the very least, to do no harm.

In society, there are many lobby groups who choose to present their viewpoints to politicians with a view to influencing decisions and legislation. Particular associations might have strongly held views, often based on their religious upbringing. Others may have come to hold passionate views based on their experiences or their thinking processes.

Whatever their basis for thinking as they do, in a democracy, it is an accepted principle, according to most national constitutions, that the majority should hold sway.[71] Generally, any change from the normal or usual experience is not something that is accepted easily by the mass of the voting people. Hence, a change of attitudes and laws is hard to achieve, particularly if it might challenge cultural or accepted ways of doing things.

The more politically confronting moral questions come from such issues as the rights of the unborn child (abortion), contraception (preventing the conceiving process from occurring) or assisted suicide (euthanasia), where the lawmakers (politicians) have been lobbied by particular interest groups who have fundamental beliefs about life and the taking of life.

One passionate lobby group in some parts of the world is the **right-to-life** or **pro-life** viewpoint. They argue against contraception, abortion and euthanasia on the basis that we shouldn't interfere with the natural processes of life and death. Frequently, this discussion has a basis in religious views – that only God should have that power – and they have a sustainable line of argument in that, from embryo to foetus, there is observable life. The proponents see themselves as advocates for the unborn. Likewise, at the end of life, they believe in nature taking its course, with palliative care being available to assist in alleviating suffering. Anything less is seen as killing human life.

On the other hand, an equally passionate viewpoint is the **right-to-choose** movement. They support the right of a woman to control her own body, her fertility and whether or not she wishes to bring a child into the world. They have equally strong views that life doesn't begin until a child is physically born – it is from the moment a child is delivered and not before.

The challenge for the pro-life movement is: How far back do you go with the definition of life in pregnancy? To conception? To a twinkle in a person's eye? This is the Sorites paradox[72] – at what point on the continuum should a child be considered to be a child? Perhaps that is why the customary definitive point of recording is the point of birth. Parish, church and civic records going back many centuries record the date of a child emerging from a mother's womb as the point of birth.

The argument that life should be recorded much earlier than birth appears to be a much more recent phenomenon.

In the late 19th century, the Catholic Church issued an encyclical called *Rerum novarum*,[73] which argued or pronounced that all life should be preserved from conception to death.

In America, in the late 19th century, most states adopted anti-abortion legislation, except when the mother's life was in danger.

By contrast, in the early 20th century, there was a movement to use **eugenics**[74] as the argument *to limit births of the poor, sexually promiscuous or mentally disabled*, especially if they were African Americans, according to Daniel K Williams, a history professor at the University of West Georgia.[75]

By the 1930s, many US doctors were arguing for less harsh anti-abortion legislation which they saw as enforcing church views on sexuality and morality – particularly, but not exclusively, from the Catholic Church.[76]

Yet, from 1939 to 1958, five US Supreme Courts and the District Court of Washington DC made rulings to endorse foetal personhood. The 1960s, in the USA, saw the first serious wave of abortion legislation across many states.

But, by 1970, times and attitudes were changing. The states of New York, Alaska and Hawaii had legislated to allow elective abortion.

In 1973, in the seminal case of *Roe v Wade*,[77] the US Supreme Court ruled that women have a constitutional right to get an abortion. In the political sphere, it remains a divisive issue until this day.

Yet, as indicated, that particular definition of the sanctity of foetal life is relatively recent in the history of views on the matter. It was on 15 May 1891 that Pope Leo XIII issued his encyclical. It was a religious edict, when the population on the planet was around 1.5 billion.

The world population passed 7 billion in 2011.[78] It was only in 1999 that the population had passed 6 billion. It had taken only 12 years to increase the world population by 1 billion; that is an increase of 1,000 million people – many of whom would and will continue to produce offspring.

That is a very different population context from the 19th century.

While medical science has reduced child deaths significantly and more people are living to child rearing age, **the arithmetic would suggest that exponential population growth on a finite planet must reach a breaking point.**

Should our rules of morality reflect this different scenario?

Likewise, with death, the advocates for **assisted death** argue that people should be allowed the dignity of deciding how they leave this life, if they are suffering from debilitating incurable illnesses. This is to spare the person unnecessary suffering which, morally and legally, we have no problem with when applying that same principle to other animals.

Suicide is not illegal. You can take your own life as long as no-one else is present. If they are, in some countries, they could be considered to be accessories in your death.

Indeed, death by suicide has been considered to be noble in many societies throughout history. Greek philosopher, Socrates, took hemlock poison to appease society's concerns about his speeches.[79] That was seen as a noble and correct action. In Japanese society, military people who failed in battle committed *harakiri*[80] to absolve shame. In Roman society, suicide was seen to be honourable – as taking responsibility.[81]

Let us return to the **context** and **the time in which we live**.

By 2025, the population of the world is projected to be 8 billion.[82]

When the Enlightenment[83] was providing much of the basis for our current moral rationale, the population was significantly less than 1 billion – indeed for the 150 years between 1650 and 1800 the world population ranged between 600 million and 900 million.[84]

Many died from illness, disease and the dangers of living. The expected average life span was around 40 years in 1800. It is now 80+ years.[85]

The context has changed.

We have become very skilled at **prolonging life** – although, it should be noted, not necessarily the quality of life. University of NSW Professor Ken Hillman is a leading intensive care doctor in 2017. With his team, he is conducting a project aimed at giving elderly patients with chronic illnesses some honest conversations about what the hospital can actually provide.

Hillman argues that many elderly people are not told the limitations of hospital treatment. *'Many of us see elderly people really lonely and suffering in hospitals when they haven't been given a choice.'* His intensive care unit is often populated by frail, aged people being kept alive (this is the law) *'even though sometimes no one knows if that's what they really want'.*[86]

These are dilemmas that doctors face daily. Ethicists also wrestle with such issues in terms of how to regulate the competing social and moral obligations, and how to advise the political system.[87]

When the dilemma is passed to the lawmakers, they must create legislation to cover end-of-life options that can be accepted by the majority of the population, albeit after being informed by ethics committees and the views of their electorates.

But sometimes, the majority population view is not enough. Politicians are also well aware that the scenario of elderly patients being legally assisted to end their lives is anathema to those who want to have **no change** to current legislation and to have a more traditional interpretation of 'dying with dignity'. Politicians are subject to electoral pressure as well as personal conscience issues.

The underlying context is that we live on a finite planet, with the powerful nations still following a colonial economic model of continual growth, based on using finite resources to fund the lifestyle of the more developed areas of the world. **That arithmetic no longer adds up, with the population of the planet expected to have increased eightfold from 1800 to 2025.**

> *Do we now have to question the type of morality which is based on tradition or on the hope that the technologies of the future will somehow manage the exponential growth of population?*

Let us briefly examine the process of how laws are made, including those regulations that will govern the behaviour of the people and reflect the morality of the time.

In democratic societies, the people vote to elect representatives who will take their views to parliament, where new laws can be crafted.

A Philosophical Morality Challenge

Each democracy has a slightly different process of election but, in essence, 'representatives' are elected from a physical area and they usually form a 'lower house' of the people – variously known by such titles as the 'House of Commons', 'The House of Assembly' or 'The House of Representatives'. It is this lower house that generates the bulk of new law proposals. In most voters' minds, each member of the lower house should be representing the views of the majority of the people who live in that electoral area.

The upper house – variously called 'The Senate', 'The Upper House' or 'The House of Lords' – is a place where proposed legislation is reviewed before it can become the law of the land, The upper house elections can take several forms; however, essentially members are selected to represent wider areas than lower house electorates, such as states or regions and to represent political interest parties – proportional representation.

Normally, legislation is voted on by the representatives in each parliamentary house and the majority vote carries the day. In principle, the elected members should be reflecting the diverse views of the community.

However, **lobby groups form another dimension to the political system.** As indicated earlier, these are particular organised advocates who seek to influence the way members might choose to vote. They do that by persuasive argument and, more pragmatically, by controlling donations to electoral campaigns – **a transparent form of bribery to sway decision makers.**

Political parties tend to meet and thrash out their common view – and then they usually vote as a block. Occasionally, the restrictions of political parties are removed and members can have a conscience vote – following their own belief systems. Sometimes, the vote is given back to the people to decide as a plebiscite for serious moral questions or as a referendum, if it requires constitutional change.

THE MOST AVOIDED QUESTIONS

Yet, doctors still have to navigate difficult moral questions on a daily basis.

Whether it be the triage process[88] of prioritising those in most need or those who can be saved/assisted or whether it is the discussion with families on when to turn off life support systems when the brain is clinically dead, doctors make these decisions while following the dictum of the Hippocratic Oath.[89]

Medical advances now help women become pregnant by In Vitro Fertilisation (IVF).[90] What is the ethical position to be on the discarding of eggs, embryos or even stored sperm? None of them can survive for long if exposed to the air and left to their own devices. It is a balance between conscience and pragmatism.

Shouldn't the laws provide supportive ethical guidelines to the medical profession which reflect the majority moral view in a democracy?

Does 'thou shalt not kill' apply to all life? Animals are bred for food and slaughtered in abattoirs. Medical science uses animals to test new developments in disease control before they are used in human trials.

Plant life is life. Is the suggestion that no plant life should be killed?

From an ecological survival viewpoint, it might be good if that policy at least applied to pristine lands and their ecosystems. Then the sustainability of the planet might get some reprieve. But, we all need to eat food of some sort to survive.

There appears to be a growth of numbers of people who are vegetarian, vegan, gluten-free or lactose-free. While some might follow that course as a result of medical conditions, others make free choices not to eat animal or wheat products.

However, the theological references, earlier in this chapter, seem to indicate that it is only human life that is prioritised.

There are also many lobby groups who want to see wildlife and domestic animals treated with respect.

> *It is interesting, however, that few people have qualms about 'putting down' sick or badly injured animals to save them from suffering, when the same compassion appears to be a moral quandary when applied to humans.*

Let us return to our moral minefield.

As we have seen from our brief historical summary, the 'right-to-life' argument is a relatively recent phenomenon, drawing its basis from particular interpretations of old theological texts or from the thinking of the Enlightenment period in history.

Even in those examples, there have been many cases throughout history and into modern times which would suggest that the notion is as much aspirational or ideological than reality (cf. wars, homicides, genocides).

The thinking behind the moral arguments of past centuries might well have been appropriate for their eras where the life expectancy was low, the availability of productive land for colonising, invading or for resource use was much greater than at present, and the models of economic growth were the unchallengeable success stories of past generations.

Now, in the 21st century, we have a high life expectancy in many parts of the world. Large areas of open space or animal habitat or limited resources are being degraded or have been lost from their earlier natural form. The bulk of world population live in cities which are divorced from the raw survival techniques of previous eras.

The economic growth models of the colonial eras are all under strain – with the disparity in world wealth being exacerbated each year.[91]

And yet, the moral priorities of those earlier eras appear to have become so entrenched that they are hard to challenge.

We might now ask several questions:

How long can the planet sustain exponential population growth before the natural ecosystems cease to function? Should that affect our perception of morality?

The planet is finite and people live within naturally-regenerating ecosystems. We have come to rely on technology to provide ways to make the supply systems more productive.

But the pressure of population, coupled with a culture of increasing demand, is straining nature's ability to reestablish from air pollution, changing climate, ocean pollution, waste disposal, over-fishing, increasingly common weather extremes and the land degrading to dust bowls or deserts.

Is it the responsibility of this generation to examine the moral foundations for the behavioural rights and responsibilities of societies across the planet?

We are the custodians of this planet for the time that we are in charge. Are we asking the hard questions about our attitudes to preserving life or a lifestyle into the future?[92]

Or, are we ignoring the *bleeding obvious* challenges because the solutions are too hard for our current political processes?

On what basis can traditional views be challenged?

It should be acknowledged that some traditional views might well be the best paths into the future, but that does not mean that they should be above questioning, testing or reassessment.

Traditions and religions are very comfortable notions. They allow people to be calm by passing responsibility onto others, either as past practice or to some deific being.

The trust and hope that a deity is controlling our lives in a way that we don't fully understand saves us from trying to explain the, as yet, unexplainable.

Religion would appear to be a natural human reaction to the complexity of the world and has been documented by social anthropologists across the globe, over time.[93] However, recent studies of history have also shown that the gods of previous civilisations (e.g. Egyptian, Greek, Roman, Viking, Aztec, Inca, Khmer … the list goes on) only tended to have deific meaning for their time and context.

We should respect people's religious beliefs. Spirituality is not always codified into particular creeds. A sense of wonder or awe is part of freedom of thought, of the joy of living.

There is also an internal human freedom that comes from believing in hope. People should be allowed to believe what they choose. But, in democracies, the constitutions set out that the majority view should carry the day with respect to social rules.

Shouldn't our laws be based on logical thinking and evidence rather than a blind belief in a religion or tradition?
If there is a logic that is not solely based on reference to the text of a belief system, then the argument should be able to be debated in the current context, using evidence which can be tested against repeatable trials to produce the same results – the scientific method can apply equally to the physical and social sciences.

Is the moral foundation of our society set in absolute terms or should it be taking note of a changing context?
The principles and values of past moral conduct operated adequately while there were natural checks and balances on population growth, food production and life style.

> *Man has now been able to transform the environment to become more productive but also more vulnerable.*

Medical advances have controlled diseases, transplanted organs and increased the understanding of hygiene. This has meant that life expectancy has more than doubled since the Enlightenment era – and the global population itself has grown by more than sevenfold from that time to the present. Technology has increased crop yields and it has modified genetics. Animal farming has become intensive.

But, food supply chains to urban areas are **dependent on energy production** – inputs in a range of forms. That system has proved to be successful ... until recently, when natural disasters have become more prevalent. The economic models of sustained growth have become strained. It is a deck of cards, waiting for one or more of the parts to falter and then societies will find it hard to manage.

The old coping techniques, from a pre-urban age, are rarely still available or even known as skills to the generations that follow.

There are over sixty-five million people who are displaced or are refugees on the planet, with no vacant or unclaimed areas for them to flee.[94] This adds to the social and political pressure at the base of the tower of cards. We shall return to the moral dilemma of refugees in a later chapter.

At what point, do we challenge the moral foundation for exponential population growth?

Is limiting the size of families a social responsibility?

Or is unlimited population growth a human right? (See Chapter 5)

The secret of happiness lies in the mind's release from worldly ties.
Buddha

Chapter 4

Is 'human nature' programmed into our DNA or is it instilled by our cultural training?

You can't take the Stone Age out of the person ... or can you?

The Harvard Business Review of 1998 published Professor Nigel Nicholson's[95] suggestion that you can't take the Stone Age out of the person.[96] Nicholson argued that some aspects of human behaviour are hardwired, particularly in how humans view survival and leadership. He is not the only writer to expound this type of view.[97]

In addition, Frans de Waal, the Dutch ethologist and scholar of primates,[98] took it one stage further to include moral behaviour. He wrote in 2013 that *'morality is natural to our species'* because he believed that he had observed it in bonobo monkeys.[99] Social anthropologists in their studies of primitive societies have consistently found similar social behavioural characteristics in terms of kinship, religion and team work. (See E. Evans Pritchard, Bronislaw Malinowski. Margaret Mead, Arthur Radcliffe Brown, amongst many.[100])

Back in the 19th century, **Charles Darwin**[101] rattled the world with his theory of natural selection. According to his theory, human beings are an evolved species, the biological descendants of a line that stretches back through apes and back to ancient simians. In fact, Darwin suggested that human beings share a common heritage with all other species.

Since Darwin's time, scientists have built on the theory of natural selection, most notably in the area of genetics. Genes that produce faulty design features – in the macro picture, at least – simply don't survive long enough in the competitive world to reproduce and pass their DNA[102] to the next generation.

That is the theory of *environmental selection.*
Nigel Nicholson argued that there have been no highly significant environmental conditions (such as a major meteorite strike) that have impacted on human survival and reproduction to the extent that our basic brain circuitry might have been forced to adapt and evolve. It still has the competitive 'survival of the fittest' mentality from early humans.

While different cultures have variations in physical characteristics (e.g. see evidence from forensic anthropology studies[103]), different languages, accepted behaviours and religious beliefs, they all appear to have **certain generic similarities** of the above, socially related to the survival of their peoples in their own contexts.

Is that nurture – taking in the peculiarities of their respective environments, and how they adapt to the demands of nature?

Grant Steen[104] covers both options as he argues that nature and nurture probably have similar proportions of input into human behaviour; that there are hereditary links to particular behaviours.

The eugenics movement[105] tried to argue that people could be trained to be better people. That thesis tended to avoid the acknowledgement that they also argued for weeding out any people who didn't fit the successful mould.

So, how much of human nature comes from training – i.e. from nurture? Is there a moral position on what the balance might be?[106]

A Philosophical Morality Challenge

The English philosopher, **John Locke**,[107] in 1690, argued that nurture was a dominant part of the development of human nature. It was the notion of the '**blank slate**' or '**tabula rasa**' onto which cultural training imbued the recipients with their characteristics. But the competing concepts of nurture vs nature go back further, to the medieval French, and have their roots in the ancient Greek thinking of good moral stories being told to children (See Chapter 1).

Locke argued that there are no innate principles in a new-born child ... or at least very few. He expounded the idea that children learn from their environment, their experience, sensations, the meanings behind words, ideas and eventually, the power of rational reasoning. He was at odds with others of his time, such as the French thinker, **Rene Descartes**,[108] who is often regarded as the 'Father of Modern Philosophy'.

Descartes was in search of absolute truth. He rejected the ideas of the 'clean slate' and that a notion of sensation could explain all human development. In his philosophical struggle, **the only certain truths for him were that 'I exist' and that there must be a power beyond that**. But Descartes rejected the Aristotle scholastic view that rooted all thinking in terms of God, which in medieval times would be interpreted as the Bible messages. He wrestled with the notion that there must be some natural roots in human development.

Locke's nurture arguments did have influential followers, such as David Hume.[109] But, in fairness, he also had many critics of his arguments, such as Leibnitz.[110] That is the nature of thoughtful debate as people search for meaning and understanding.

> ***These types of philosophical ponderings and arguments are important because they have conditioned the debates around how moral philosophy and ethics have developed in Western thinking***

To that extent, Western cultures have demonstrated serious respect for the writers of the Enlightenment because they provided a non-theological basis for positioning in rational debates about morality.

Yet, Chinese culture might suggest that modern Western moral thinking still owes a lot of its basis to the influence of the religions based on Abraham (Judaism, Christianity and Islam) which are all based around their interpretations of one absolute truth around one God, monotheism (although it is accepted that not all scholars agree with that Western monotheism notion, cf. Levenson.[111])

As history has shown, the Abrahamic religions have been prepared to fight for, and to protect, the emblems of their own particular stance on absolute truth – thus influencing the priorities and policies of many nations, over decades and centuries.

By contrast, in China, Daoism (based on the philosophies of Lao Tze or Laozi[112]), Confucianism (based on sayings of Kongzi – Confucius[113] – a disciple of Laozi) and Buddhism (based on Siddhartha Gautama's teaching in the late 6th century BCE – Buddha[114]) all appear to operate in *Hé* (harmony), a non-aggressive acceptance of each other, because those religions are about relationships with other people rather than the individual seeking a single truth.

Is this an argument for the nurture of peoples' thinking – an Eastern way of operating and an expository Western way?
The thinking in the Dao De Jing[115] of Laozi is subtle, like a gerund (an -ing word, a verb acting as modifying noun) rather than a definitive straight noun (a naming word).

If nurture can produce such diverse ways of thinking, what is the commonality from the donation of nature?
Perhaps nature provides the root similarities of physical characteristics which can be modified by location, time and context. That is,

the arguments for a moral approach to social responsibility/ways of behaving are inculcated within the traditions of particular cultures.

If there are fundamental human behaviours which are common to humans, how much of that is inherited in a genetic code?
Studies of DNA[116] would suggest that there are significant similarities as the basis of all genetic codes.[117] The similarity proportion appears to contribute a large part of the code.

Doesn't that imply that the nurture aspect is smaller?
That bland use of numbers doesn't take into account the significance of the weighting of each influence. Surely a simplistic proportion approach would misrepresent the power of human thinking to influence development and adaptability?

Dr Beben Benjamin at the University of Queensland, Australia, reviewed almost every study into twins over the past fifty years – that is 14.5 million twin pairs and found that the discussion should be about nature *and* nurture because just less than half of the human traits are genetic with 51 per cent being environmental factors (or measurement error). However, he did find that the risk of contracting certain diseases, such as bipolar disorder, was 70 per cent genetic.[118]

How much does environment (upbringing, schooling, education, circumstance) contribute to attitude and morality?
This is an interesting question because it implies that conformity to the training and education within a culture is both good and right (moral). However, the differences in cultures can refine such beliefs and understandings to be polar opposites of each other (as illustrated in earlier chapters).

Berger and Luckmann, in *The Social Construction of Reality*, present the thesis that no human thought is immune from the ideological influences of its social context. They note that even in the organisational change of companies, it is important to understand the individual's social construction of reality.[119] That becomes particularly important when applied to business attitudes towards wealth or the lack of it. (See later chapters.)

From a morality viewpoint, we can ask,
How much of our moral attitudes are entrenched in tradition? That is the argument that 'it has always been so' and therefore must represent the truth of its rightness.

Bertrand Russell, in *On Education* in 1926 (p.127),[120] wrote: *A truly robust morality can only be strengthened by the fullest knowledge of what **really** happens in the world.* That is very different from an aspirational view of morality. Russell was a Nobel laureate for literature as well as being a professor of mathematics and philosophy. In essence, he challenged many of the irrefutable assumptions of society which to him appeared to be accepted just because that was the way it had always been.

One of the challenges in listening to group attitudes about morality is to differentiate between consensus[121] and groupthink.[122] The differences are subtle to the casual observer and yet the influence could be seen as beneficial or detrimental depending on your viewpoint.

Consensus suggests that there is a considered acceptance of a group view, having had fair appreciation of all opinions and evidence. Groupthink implies an intimidation which encourages some participants to remain quiet rather than express their opposing viewpoints or to challenge the supremacy of the powerful.

Consequently, your social context can be manipulated to influence attitudes and morality.

We shall return to this concept.

A great man is sparing in words but prodigal in deeds.
Confucius

Chapter 5

Are parents responsible for their children?

At the most fundamental level, if you bring a child into the world, as the parent, you take a responsibility to raise that child until it is independent.

For legal purposes that transition stage is normally established as 18 years of age. That parental responsibility would be a common perception, albeit acknowledging an African proverb that *it takes a village to raise a child*.[123]

The antithesis of that responsibility view is when the result of an act of copulation eventually brings a child into the world and it is the expectation of the parents that society/the government should fund and, in some cases, rear the child; and any number of future children.

That is an extrapolation of the child support scheme[124] – a welfare system which exists in many developed countries to protect the interests of children, irrespective of who their parents might be. The support scheme is a government policy construct which stems from a community/political humanitarian view – a moral view if you like – that all children in certain developed countries should have the resources to give them a good start in life.

A former Australian treasurer, Peter Costello, when introducing the *baby bonus* – a government financial incentive for parents to have children – suggested that parents should have one child for each of them and one more for the country.[125] It is probable that he was viewing his policy from an economic angle that more children would eventually become more tax payers and purchasers for the retail market. This approach, however, only works if 'the more' children eventually engage in that work, pay taxes and are not dependent on society. Otherwise, it increases welfare costs with no net benefit to the economy.

A further responsibility of the parents is to ensure that the children receive the education and training necessary to become independent adult citizens in their communities.

The type of training will vary across cultures and nationalities but, nevertheless, it is a social expectation that parents would assist their children to become active and independent members of the community.

At the risk of taking a philosophical questioning into the minefield of ideologies, it is important to note the importance of people having jobs or meaningful occupation.[126] Roy Baumeister and Mark Leary are among many who have published research showing that there is human need to have a sense of social worth, of belonging.[127] Marylene Gagne has edited a range of research on the psychological need for the social groupings that are provided by work, of having the independence of income to make their own family decisions about how people live and how they can spend any leisure time.[128]

Those priorities should transcend political ideologies and should prioritise the value of being employed or in business or in valued community activity, especially as automation and technological advances change the traditional workplace roles.

Is there a need for a cultural reform in our attitudes to the priority of meaningful work?

When automation replaces some work roles, should there be a requirement for the business or society to generate different work roles to keep people gainfully employed/socially involved and not dependent on others, using the logic of the research above?

Across the world, what are some of the cultural factors for rearing large families?

Let us examine the reasons and attitudes which are contributing to the exponential growth of world population? Some of them are part of cultural morality,

> *In previous eras, there was a need to have large families in the hope that some children would survive to child-rearing age.*

Life expectancy rates in the 17th century were under 40 years, largely due to high infant mortality.[129] An average English woman of that time would give birth six or seven times and many children would not reach the age of majority.

Currently, in Burkino Faso, 8.9 per cent of children will die before their fifth birthday. In Haiti, it is 6.7 per cent, as compared to Australia with 0.4 per cent.[130]

In areas of no pensions or social security benefits, children are needed to care for the elderly – and that need becomes ingrained in the developing culture of the societies.

A lack of effective contraception is another significant factor.

Development is the best contraceptive

Dr Karan Singh, an Indian government minister, made the statement at the World Population Conference in Bucharest in 1974, that *'development is the best contraceptive'*.[131] He was arguing for a social environment that is more conducive to reducing the fertility rate – more secondary education to delay teenage marriages and to change community attitudes so that women would be valued for more than their child-rearing function.

In many parts of the world, the number of children has reduced significantly in recent years, perhaps due to better contraception options or government legislation as in the case of China with its one child policy from 1979 to 2015.[132]

China has announced a slackening of that policy from 2016 but **the cultural change has happened** with many couples choosing to have only one child or none at all. The effect has been to reduce the average number of children per woman in that huge population of China from 6.5 to 1.5 over the period of the policy and it is still continuing.

> *Demographic studies in Ghana, Ethiopia and Kenya show a clear correlation of lower birth rates for women with progressively more years of education.*[133]

This might suggest that higher levels of education are giving women more options in life, more status in the community, and an awareness of the wider world so they are delaying the birth of a first child for months and years. The *United Nations Educational, Scientific and Cultural Organisation* (UNESCO) estimates that 60 per cent fewer teenage girls in sub-Saharan Africa would become pregnant **early** if they had a secondary education.[134]

The effect of religions who preach against contraception can have a large influence on birth rates. For example, Latin America has a very large following of Catholic Church pronouncements, one of which is not to use contraception (See Chapter 3).[135]

> *Custom plays a significant role in affecting birth rates within countries with a dominant male culture.*

The social pressure to subject girls to early marriage and women to continually produce children can be seen as a **community status symbol** in countries with a dominant male culture. Beals[136] noted that a large household in his study village of Golapur in India was seen as being prestigious for the man of the house; a sign of his success in life. Colliver[137] in his study of the Jie people of Uganda noted that Jie marriage is primarily about procreation and that a marriage is not confirmed until the birth and survival of children.

The notion of the **harem**[138], whose purpose was to produce offspring for wealthy leaders, is associated with the Abbabid caliphs of Baghdad (750–1258 CE), Ottoman sultans (1300–1923 CE), Safavid (1501–1732 CE) and Mughal ruling class (1526–1739 CE).

Cultures which view women as chattels are the most likely to set rules which ensure that women do not have the same rights as men, that they are adjuncts to men (as wives or other terminologies) and are obliged to be sexual and childbearing possessions. Until relatively recently in human history, that attitude would have been very common across the planet. It persists, supported by religious cultures, particularly in parts of India, the Middle East, Africa and Latin America.[139]

The use of **rape** in warring situations has been a practice over the centuries, where women were seen as property of the vanquished and therefore they were a valid entitlement for the victors, who acquired the property as an accepted part of plunder.

The 1949 Fourth Geneva Convention, Article 27, explicitly prohibits wartime rape and enforced prostitution in international conflicts.[140] But it continues this day, as with the Yasidi women in Iraq who have been held and sold as sex slaves from 2016 until the present.[141] And it continues in peacetime situations too.[142]

So, we return to the question of children and who is responsible for them.

On 20 November 1959, the General Assembly of the United Nations adopted Geneva Declaration of the Rights of the Child of 1924 and the Declaration of the Rights of the Child.

The principles are recognised both in the International Covenant on Civil and Political Rights and in the Universal Declaration of Human Rights. In particular, Articles 23 and 24 are concerned with the welfare of children.[143] At an international convention level, there is a requirement on signatory nations to ensure that children are cared for responsibly.

Yet, there are many children in slavery or sweat shops across the world. Can that be so?
The International Labour Organisation (ILO) estimates that in 2012 there were 5.5 million children in slavery, trafficking, debt bondage and other forms of forced labour, forced recruitment for armed conflict, prostitution, pornography and other illicit activities.[144] That figure does not include many more millions in the economic slavery of child labour.

As with many moral questions, the need to look after the innocents is often at odds with the need to hold parents accountable for the children that they bring into the world.

> ***The child didn't ask to be born and had no say as to where, when and to whom he/she was born.***

Yet, there is the human compassion of the village to help rear the child.

In developed countries, **Children's Courts** generally require parents of misbehaving children to attend court and take responsibility for their erring offspring.

In an increasing number of cases, **children are taken into care** for their own safety. Then they are placed with foster families or institutions. In both Britain and Australia, the increase has been up to

15 per cent per year.[145] In England, in March 2016, there were 70,400 children being 'looked after' in various types of care. The history of institutional care is littered with significant occurrences of abuse across many nations. (See Royal Commission into Institutional Child Abuse in Australia.[146] It is but one recent example in one country.)

We return to the moral question – the question of right and wrong – after our scan across the history of attitudes to rising population, estimated to reach 8 billion by 2025.

Are we entitled to ask why so many children are being born when the need is to maintain or reduce the population of the world, to alleviate the strain on ecosystems?

In response, while the population of the world increased by 400 per cent in the 20th century, the projection is that in the 21st century it might only increase by 50 per cent and with the bulk of the growth anticipated to be in Africa.[147] But that is still a very large number, with more than 7 billion as the starting base number for exponential growth.

Is there a moral assumption that fertility rates are matters of human rights and that a woman should be able to choose to have as many children as she wishes?

Or are there parameters in this time and context – such as, if you have those children, you must be able to support them to independence?

Does that attitude then favour the wealthy over the poor? Or the free women over the oppressed?

There are sixty-five million refugees or displaced people in the world with very few places to which they can flee.

Does that context of conflict and over-population suggest the need for the implementation of national and international policies, such as higher levels of education, availability of contraception and the rights of the woman, rather than the man, to choose whether or not to have children?

That is the moral dilemma of this much avoided question.

*Vision without action is a daydream.
Action without vision is a nightmare.*

Japanese proverb

Chapter 6

Do only some belief systems have the answers for the future? Whether or not that is correct, why is it important?

> *Religion has been part of social culture for as long as can be identified by anthropological studies.*

Let us be clear at the outset that there is nothing wrong with people believing in some celestial or deific being. From ancient tribes, through waves of invading civilisations to modern times, some form of religion has been a mechanism for Man being able to accept the unexplainable – to make a kind of sense of the order that appears in the natural world or the broader universe.

Certainly, over the centuries, religious views have changed. For example, witchcraft amongst the Azandi[148] is viewed today with a similar intellectual tolerance as with the sun god of the Incas.[149]

Some religions have continued for thousands of years or, at least, have their roots back in those times. Other belief systems are much more modern, products of the last century or two.

For many people, belief brings a sense of peace, of hope for the future. Indeed, certain aspects of prophetic thought **have inspired** the development of moral thinking in civilisations — how people should treat one another; how the social order should work.

Some of the most remarkable buildings on Earth were built to acknowledge religious beliefs. That is why we can wonder at the architectural skills of cathedral and mosque builders, the constructors of pyramids in Egypt and Central America, or the monasteries and temples of Tibet, Bhutan, Myanmar, Laos, India, Cambodia, China and Europe.

Religion has been the stimulation for so much of classical music and painting which the world has enjoyed over centuries.

The challenge with belief systems is that they are based on human interpretation; and those interpretations can affect the broader laws of the lands in which we live.

They can become codified and revered as *the only true way* which then limits the need for people to think further. **That is why they are important.**

Taoism or Daoism is based on the Dao De Jing, the verses of Laozi, from 200 BCE. It has continued for over 2000 years.[150] Most proponents of that belief system would acknowledge that there are several translations of the messages which were passed on verbally, initially, from Laozi.

Further, followers of the Dao De Jing are quick to observe that words are an inadequate method of communicating spiritual meaning. At best, they are someone's interpretation. Most favour the notion of images rather than words or verse to convey feelings and senses. They speak of intuition rather than logical processes.

In the **Christian religion**, the Bible has been translated many times in genuine attempts to record meaning from gospels, parables and the Old Testament stories.[151] Inevitably, the interpreters see meaning through the eyes of their own time and contexts as they try to transfer understanding from language to language, era to era, so as to make the revered texts meaningful to their generations (cf. King James Version started in 1604 and finished in 1611;[152] and New International Version, written in the 1970s and updated in 2011[153]).

This is a bit like the challenge of Daoism that words can mean many things, depending on who is reading them. It is not surprising, then, that there are many denominations of most religions as people seek to find the interpretations that resonate for them and are perhaps different from the mainstream in their approach.

While the main arms of Christianity might be Catholic and Protestant, the list of Christian denominations runs to many hundreds across the globe,[154] all of which consider themselves to be valid translations of the word of God.

The Bible, as the foundation document, was written over at least a 1,500 year period.[155] Possibly the earliest date for the Old Testament is around 600 BCE, based on some inscribed shards of pottery.[156] The list of contributors to the final Bible is extensive; by at least forty different authors over a long time span.[157] There is a full range of opinions about when and by whom the New Testament was written.[158] Irrespective of when, how and by whom it has been recorded, it is the interpreted message of the Bible on which the religion is based.

The religion of **Islam**, the world's second largest religion, has variations of understanding such as Sunni (87–90 per cent), Shia (10–13 per cent),[159] with other minor offshoots, such as Sufi. Its foundation document is the Qu'ran. Muslims believe that its content was revealed orally to the prophet, Mohammed, from 610–632 CE, by the Angel Gabriel.[160] Ulthman, the third caliph (644–656 CE) produced the first written Qu'ran from the recollections of disciples at the time.

Hinduism claims to be the third largest religion in the world. It is most common in India and Nepal. It is founded on *Santana*

Dharma, a fusion or synthesis of ethical ideas stemming from at least 500 BCE. It has four main currents – Vishnu, Shiva, Devi and Smartism. Hinduism has no founder, no prophets and no binding holy book.[161]

Buddhism has three main branches – Theravada, Mahayana and Vajrayana or Tantric. Theravada stems from the oldest texts set down in Pali language in Sri Lanka in the first century CE. The others are revisions or reforms.[162] Buddhism lays claim to being the fourth largest religion in the world.

Judaism has three main movements – Orthodox, Reform and Conservative – with many sub-lines within their practices.[163] It claims its origin in the 8th century BCE. Its foundation manuscript is the Hebrew Bible, plus 'the law' or Torah, a collection of religious and ethical guidelines.

The recent centuries have produced many new religions. Some are sects (offshoots of established religions, such as the Church of Latter Day Saints)[164] or are based on new foundations, such as Scientology.[165]

Even this brief scan over world religions reveals the diversity and scope of the beliefs which people in the world have every right to hold.

The challenge for morality comes when the laws of nations are based on particular religions for their sole justification.

Large parts of the Western world have laws which draw heavily on Judeo-Christian traditions. Other large areas of the world have laws based on Sharia, the Muslim tradition. While they are each religions based on Abraham, as we have already indicated, the interpretations of meaning can be very different, even opposing, particularly if fundamentalist (or extremist) views are taken.

A Philosophical Morality Challenge

When seeking a moral standard in legislation, it largely depends on the governance structures for particular nations. When disagreement on religious answers can be so divergent across the world, then it is hard for organisations like the United Nations to come up with universal standards.

The former UN Secretary-General, Ban ki Moon, wrote about the Universal Declaration of Human Rights (UDHR) that:

The extraordinary vision and resolve of the drafters produced a document that, for the first time, articulated the rights and freedoms to which every human being is equally and inalienably entitled.

Now available in more than 360 languages, the Declaration is the most translated document in the world – a testament to its global nature and reach. It has become a yardstick by which we measure right and wrong. It provides a foundation for a just and decent future for all, and has given people everywhere a powerful tool in the fight against oppression, impunity and affronts to human dignity.[166]

The 1948 UDHR has been adopted by many countries but not everyone shares Ban ki Moon's confidence about its status as a global yardstick measure of right and wrong. Several significant world areas did not sign up in 1948, particularly the then Soviet Union and some of its satellites, as well as Saudi Arabia and South Africa.

Indeed, in 1982, the Iranian representative to the United Nations said that the Declaration was *a secular understanding of the Judeo-Christian tradition* which could not be implemented by Muslims without conflict with Sharia.[167]

On 30 June 2000, members of the Organisation of the Islamic Conference officially resolved to support the Cairo Declaration on Human Rights in Islam (first adopted in principle in 1990).[168] This is an alternative document that says people have *freedom and right to a dignified life in accordance with the Islamic Shari'ah*, without any discrimination on grounds of *race, colour, language, sex, religious belief, political affiliation, social status or other considerations*.

To illustrate, its main variations state that, *All men are equal in terms of basic human dignity (but not equal human rights).* Furthermore, it gives women certain rights but not equal rights, in general. Men and women are given unequal rights to marry a non-Muslim, to marry more than one spouse or to divorce their spouses. Essentially, the restrictions are all seen to be in accordance with the interpretations of Sharia.

So, from a moral viewpoint, nations which adhere to the two major religions on the planet are coming from opposing viewpoints with respect to the detail of human rights. These Declaration documents are major international statements which are intended to be entrenched in the national laws of their signatories. They are, to a smaller or greater extent, based on religious interpretations of the foundation documents of their respective faiths.

> *The significance of religious beliefs is that they influence the decision makers in debates and in conscience votes on matters of moral or ethical complexity.*

From a moral perspective, we can now ask:

What areas of common ground would be shared by the opposing opinions on human rights?

The two major religions both appear to generally accept human dignity and no discrimination on the basis of race, language, religion, sex, politics or social status. A main sticking point comes with attitudes to the rights of women.

Let us now consider the situation of Africa.

> *Africa faces many challenges around human rights and a range of belief systems.*

What is the moral solution to Africa's challenges around population expansion, human rights and belief systems?

The African experience of colonialism and military rule in many of its countries has led to a repression of criticism or rational critiquing. Free participation in several countries is prevented by political intimidation.

The challenges should also not ignore the long slave trade history which has plundered the human wealth and confidence of the continent's societies for centuries and, possibly, millennia.[169]

Kwasi Wiredu, an African philosopher,[170] writes of the colonial period being a political imposition, and also a cultural one, particularly with the introduction of colonial languages to the detriment of distinctive African thinking and tribal processes. Wiredu promotes a particularly African approach of the village culture embracing their global past and future.

Also in Africa, Yusef Waghid[171] writes of the positive role that education and a philosophical/moral framework can, and should, play in the face of not only the significant challenges of famine, hunger, poverty, abuse and violence but also the prevalence of military dictatorships.

Under military rule, the institutions require that people 'toe the line'. Coercion and control take away the room for dissent or democratic engagement. And yet, the African philosophy of education that Waghid speaks about is **geared towards justice, freedom and democratic processes.**

Such an approach has happened with noted success in some African countries, particularly South Africa, Tanzania and Zambia. These examples could well provide the momentum for other African countries to move from the subjugation of the people to one where the population can provide analyses and responses to the legitimate concerns of many people on the continent.

It should be noted that when the UN UDHR was signed in 1948, most of the countries of Africa were under the colonial control of one or other of the several European colonial countries and, consequently, had no vote at the United Nations. Through the 1960s and onwards, many of the African countries gained their political independence and are now signatories to the UDHR. However, **political and corruption-free stability has taken much longer** in so many countries which have had their borders drawn across multiple tribal areas.

According to Waghid and other African writers, the grassroots movement for independence needs to provide the educational opportunities for its people to learn, to listen, to reflect and to reason. Then they could critique the military and terrorist power which can control so much of their lives. That military power is also likely sponsored with weapons from the developed countries which still rely on Africa for their resources.

From a moral standpoint – a sense of right or wrong – surely, after such a history of plunders and coercion, it should be the role of the people in particular countries to resolve how they wish to govern and be governed. While there is a need to rid the thinking of corruption and to protect the vulnerable from violence, it is not the role of outsiders, with particular viewpoints and vested interests, to impose their perspectives on others. **That was the process of colonisation – and it smacks of self-righteousness.**

Is self-righteous rule morally right? Or is it used to hide other agendas?

Many monarchs have claimed to rule under **the divine right of kings.**[172] That claim asserts that the monarch is subject to no earthly authority, deriving the right to rule directly by the will of God. That justification usually channels Biblical references to God, who apparently chose kings to rule over Israel.

But a similar principle is also found in Aryan and Egyptian cultures.

Indeed, sultans in Asia claimed divine or heavenly right to rule, as did the emperors of Japan and China. Such pronounced claims were generally entrenched in community belief systems by the social teachings of their cultures, so that the ruler's rights were accepted without question.

Those religious maxims originated centuries ago and enabled dynasties to stay in power, within certain parameters. At least from the outside looking back, **the maintenance of power would appear to be a major motivator in keeping the status quo.**

However, if the ruling powers flaunted their power such that they ignored the wishes and trials of the majority, different events in history have shown that, in time, even the divine right of the powerful elite might well be challenged, forcing the rulers to either adapt or be overthrown.

Power and privilege can blind the self-righteous.

It can be hard for self-entitled rulers to see beyond the narcissistic world of their own endorsement ... or to imagine walking in the shoes of those that they rule. Then, they suffer utter disbelief when they are deposed – often fatally.

For example, the French aristocracy didn't see it coming in the 18th century.[173] The Romanovs in Russia didn't see it coming in the 20th century.[174] Charles I of England didn't see it coming in the 17th century [175] nor did the dictator, Ceaușescu, in Romania in 1989.[176] However, in each case – as with many, revolutions and civil wars – it changed the way that those countries were governed.

Is the working solution for all countries to be aware of the opposing viewpoints and to treat each other with respect?
The experience of history has been that one group or the other will generally try to assert its power over the rest.

For example, the expansion of the Arab empire in the years following the Prophet Muhammad's death (632 CE) led to the creation of caliphates occupying a large geographical area from India to the

Atlantic. Conversion to Islam was boosted by the missionary work of imams who intermingled easily with the local populace to propagate the religious teachings.

That process is not significantly different from Christian missionaries taking Christianity and their version of civilisation to the people in their colonised countries.

But it was Muslim economics and trading, coupled to the later expansion of the Ottoman Empire, which led to some of the most powerful Muslim empires in the world from the Atlantic coast to India, and even latterly into South-East Asia.[177] The people of the Islamic world created numerous sophisticated centres of culture and science with far-reaching mercantile networks, travellers, scientists, mathematicians, doctors and philosophers, all contributing to the Golden Age of Islam.[178] This lasted from the 8th to the 13th centuries CE. (See Chapter 7)

The medieval Christian Crusades from the 11th to the 13th centuries were religious wars, sanctioned by the Latin church, ostensibly to reclaim holy sites from Islamic control.[179] So, **both groups have shown expansionist ideals rather than mutual respect for one another.**

That ethnocentric approach to the resolution of cultural differences led to conflict right into the 20th century, with Western powers dividing up Middle East lands without regard to customary practice. That situation has not been resolved even into the 21st century. (See Chapter 2)

Notwithstanding, the powerful influence of religions over national and international agendas throughout history, **care should be taken to not just see the challenges of religions**.

At a local through to international level, people imbued with the virtues of religious faith frequently do contribute significantly to many needy people in society with their good deeds.

A Philosophical Morality Challenge

Alain de Botton, writer, philosopher and professed atheist,[180] writes about the dangers of a secular society focusing everything on self, on Man's ability to solve life's problems through science or technology alone. Religions have helped develop certain positive aspects in the dynamics of the societies in which we live.

He sees that, even for the disbeliever in religious doctrine or creeds, there should be a human recognition of the compassionate and ethical social behaviour of some religious organisations. Service agencies, affiliated to major religions, are frequently among the first-on-call at disasters, in war zones or urban tragedies – with a mission to help.

Is the reliance on religious interpretations a function of the type of governance of nations?
Very probably.

Muslim countries take parts of their legal systems and governance styles from their interpretations of Sharia. Majority Christian countries tend to follow a more democratic approach, with some of the legal precedents drawn from Biblical messages or vestiges of old theological principles. Many religions are male dominated and those attitudes can affect the way laws are developed, particularly with respect to the rights of women.

From the 19th century onwards, countries with primarily male-dominated governance rules and at least lip-service to democratic systems have frequently shown rejection of the principles of equal rights (as understood in the UDHR).

So, yes, interpretations of religions can influence the governance of countries.

Self-righteousness has also been a belief and a guise to maintain power and control the development of public policy. Corruption, intimidation and manipulation of voting have often been characteristics in many nations, where the leadership seeks to entrench power in the hands of a dynastic few, a political elite or a military junta (e.g. North Korea, Zimbabwe, Myanmar).

But **the pursuit of power can shield itself behind many deceptions.** It is not just the prerogative of *deluded villains in other lands*. Without adequate social checks and balances against the abuse of influence, the lure of arrogant control can affect ruling groups in most countries, as later chapters might suggest.

Hope is as hollow as fear.
Laozi

Chapter 7

Were the Dark Ages really dark?

The term 'Dark Ages' was first coined by an Italian Petrarch, in 1330 CE. He was saddened by the loss of a Latin culture since the Roman era.[181] But the term was re-created by English and European writers of the 16th century onwards, who viewed the history of their world in three phases:

- The first or Classical phase describes the Greek and Roman expansion in thinking, architecture and art; which ended around 500 CE.
- A third phase started with the Renaissance (16th century CE) where, in the view of western European writers, enlightened thought, science, mathematics, art and trading prosperity had returned.
- The second phase was 'the Dark Ages' – the period of centuries in between – where there was political turmoil, social unrest, a lack of academic disciplines, a spread of diseases like the bubonic plague. The notion of cultural development, in the view of the 16th century writers, was on hold during this time.

Clearly, this was the ethnocentric position from the people who saw the first and third phases as an acceptable standard for civilised development.

They also viewed the part in between as a dark and miserable time, from their perspective, and they generally omitted anything positive from their narrative about that era.

And yet …

The time span of the 'Dark Ages' saw the rise of Charlemagne (768–814 CE), the expansion of the art, culture and exploration of the Vikings and the Golden Age of Islam, amongst others.

Charlemagne was a Frankish warrior king who fought battles from southern Spain to eastern Germany, as well as parts of Italy and Bohemia. He united them under one reign. In 800 CE, Pope Leo III crowned Charlemagne as the Holy Roman Emperor. Many nobles lost much of their near absolute power under that rule, but peasants were encouraged to participate in the marketplace and they had some improvement in freedom. Charlemagne promoted literacy in Latin and encouraged Christianity. Trading was stabilised under one currency. For a while, there was reform and a common sense of belonging.

The **Vikings** used a system of writing known as the runic alphabet or *futhark*. The runes are 'engravings' which connect to a whole system of Norse mythology. The Vikings developed the longboat which enabled them to travel the oceans and rivers from 800–1000 CE. They explored, traded and settled from Norway to Scotland, England, Iceland, Greenland, Ireland, Vinland and through the rivers into Russia and the Middle East.

For two hundred years, the Vikings were a dominant force in trading, politics and warfare. They developed an expertise in navigating, even through fog conditions.[182] They clarified the English taxation system and introduced their own currency to replace the bartering, which had been prevalent in England since the coinage of Roman times. There are many Norse words incorporated into the

English language – such words are *window, gang, angry, law* and *thrust* as well as many place names.

The Vikings helped spread the idea of commerce; of western Europe trading with the Middle East and with Mediterranean Arab Caliphates.

The reputation of the Vikings was also as vicious and successful warriors who traded consistently in slaves (that brought high prices in the human labour world), fish, wool and leather in return for spices, jewellery, silks, wine, amber and pottery. They used silver and gold coins which spread across their many areas of influence.

Waldemar Januszcsak, a British art critic, in his four-part BBC documentary on The Dark Ages,[183] emphasised the incredible art which was produced by the much maligned barbarian Huns,[184] Vandals,[185] and Goths.[186] In his view, these cultures were well-developed, produced high-quality art work and their lifestyles have been largely ignored in the modern world by reducing the memory of them, in derogatory terms, to mere warlike tribes.

The **Golden Age of Islam** usually refers to a period from the Abbasid caliphate (786–809 CE) until the sack of Baghdad by the Mongol invasion in 1258 CE.[187] That period is renowned for the flourishing of science, economic development and cultural works. Under this Islamic rule, algebra and algorithms developed significantly. Moslem art made great use of a variety of geometric shapes (rhombus, hexagons, bow ties, pentagons) linked by straplike shapes known as girih.[188]

- Ibn Muʿādh al-Jayyānī (989–1079 CE) lived in Andalusia in Spain. He wrote commentaries on Euclid's Elements and took them to a new level with his work on **spherical trigonometry**, notably with the law of sines.[189]
- Ibn al-Haytham (965–1040 CE), also known as Alhazen, was a scientist who lived near Cairo in the Fatimid caliphate. He is credited with developing the techniques of

experiment, particularly with **optics and astronomy,** and the notion that hypotheses must be confirmable by repeatable trials – **the scientific method.**[190] Alhazen also developed the sum formula for the fourth power which he used to calculate the volume of the paraboloid.

- Muhammad ibn Zakariya al-Razi (854–925 CE), also known as Rhazes, lived in Persia. He built **a classification system for chemicals** and used it to develop experimental medicine. He wrote a pioneering book about the diseases of smallpox and measles. Through translation, his works have greatly influenced the thinking in western universities, centuries later. He has been variously described as 'the doctor's doctor', **'the father of pediatrics'** and 'the pioneer of ophthalmology'.[191]

The Fatimid era (909–1171 CE) is renowned for promotion of art and literature, as well as its tolerance of free speech, provided that the speakers did not infringe on other people's rights.[192] The Fatimid era ended when they were invaded by Saladin.[193]

Islamic art of this era was characterised by distinctive ceramics (known as lustreware), glasswork, metalwork, woodwork and textiles. In addition, in literature, the illuminated manuscripts and texts[194] of those times have become a much respected art form using impressive colouring techniques and distinctive calligraphy.

Much of the literature from the Classical period was translated from Greek and Latin into Arabic. The preservation of Greek and Roman texts and the maintenance of that literary link should acknowledge the fine efforts of these Islamic scribes.[195]

So, from a moral viewpoint, what does this information say about the 'Dark Ages'?

Perhaps, it is emphasising our hypothesis which is that morality is a product of its time and context.

A Philosophical Morality Challenge

The terminology, 'the Dark Ages', is an ethnocentric classification of its time which also chooses to ignore or 'put down' the significant enlightened thought that was happening throughout the non Anglo-Saxon parts of Europe before the much-vaunted Enlightenment of Britain, France and Germany from the 16th century onwards.

We might postulate that the rich culture in the rest of Europe from the 6th to the 15th centuries did not fit with the narrative of nations who were by then setting out to colonise the rest of the world. But a scan of the evidence in this short chapter alone should show that any pejorative term used about that period was possibly an attempt to manipulate history to fit the image of the new all-conquering colonists.

Is that right or wrong in terms of a moral approach to knowledge and understanding?

*O wad some power, the gift tae gie us
Tae see ourselves as ithers see us.*

Robert Burns (Scotland's national bard)

Chapter 8

Is it right to accumulate as much wealth as you can?

How rich are the richest people really?

- In 2014, Oxfam warned that the richest eighty-four people in the world had as much wealth as the poorest 3.5 billion.[196] You can fit eighty-four people on a double-decker bus, at a pinch – while 3.5 billion is greater than the combined populations of China, India, USA, Indonesia, Brazil and Nigeria.[197]
- In 2015, Credit Suisse released their Global Wealth Report[198] confirming that 1 per cent of the world's population (mainly leaders of global corporations) controlled half of the world's wealth.
- In 2017, Christine Lagarde, the head of the International Monetary Fund, announced that the eight richest people in the world (multi-billionaires) control as much wealth as half the world's poorest – 3.6 billion people.[199] You could fit those eight in a limousine, without a pinch.

Why is this so?

Lagarde's view of this global wealth disparity, which she has been proclaiming for four years, is:[200]

'With lower growth, more inequality and much more transparency, you have the good ingredients for a crisis of the middle classes in the advanced economies.'

She doesn't advocate walking away from globalisation but adds that policy makers need to engage in a granular mix of policies designed to stimulate activity and ensure that the fruits of growth are more evenly spread.

We shall unpack that suggestion a little, during the chapter.

It should be clear from the data and commentary above that the economic models in use at present suggest a pyramidic economic structure which is being well-used to the advantage of international corporations. That process allows vast amounts of money to be passed up the system, as royalties, commission or tribute, at the expense of the majority of the people who are doing the lower-paid work at the base level.

The economic models that we use today are still based on historic colonial models of invasion and exploitation.

The colonial economic models were designed to access land and people, as well as industrial and agricultural resources. Most of the benefit was intended to return to the entrepreneurs in the mother countries.

In the late 18th and early 19th centuries, Napoleon's armies conquered most of Europe and parts of North Africa – colonising large areas on behalf of France, bringing a justice system and commercial order. His victorious armies had **permission to have a share in any plunder or loot in the conquered areas**, because Napoleon believed that his troops were underpaid and this was a fair means of recompense.[201]

He was following an age-old tradition from the earliest tribes, to the Persians, Alexander the Great, the Romans and the Mongols, right through to Nazis in World War II and even the Coalition of the

Willing in the late 20th century, in a more subtle effort to influence oil reserves.[202]

The European colonial empires from the 17th century onwards had Spain and Portugal going into South America. Britain and France competed with Spain in North America for control of land, mines and plantations. The same countries were active in Africa, with Germany, the Netherlands and Belgium, in seeking access to the resources of people, mining and agriculture.

The Dutch colonised the East Indies – present-day Indonesia.

Britain extended its 19th century influence to India, Malaya, Singapore, Hong Kong, Australia and New Zealand as well as a number of Pacific and Caribbean islands to form *'an empire on which the sun never sets'*.[203]

The narrative of those times was about bringing civilisation and religion to the colonised countries. But the underlying agenda was about commerce and the strategic positioning of defence forces.[204]

The commercial companies traded in everything from slaves, rubber, teak, tobacco, exotic spices, textiles (like cotton and jute) … through to gold, silver and the metals for the industrial revolution. In return, the colonies provided a ready market for the products of the mother countries, such as finished textiles and engineering products, like boats and railway lines – all of which helped the spiral into dependence for the colonised lands.

The only way such large empires could be maintained at a distance was through military might – hence the need for strategic bases across their domains, to show an organised armed presence.

Meanwhile, large country houses, mansions and chateaux were built as status symbols in the mother countries for the beneficiaries of the industrial, political and military power.

The model of the wealth flowing towards those who made the rules has continued to this day through the legal systems of royalties, the economies of scale and political education systems which promote the virtues of capital and the accumulation of wealth.

Meanwhile, the people at the base of the system were schooled into an unquestioning belief of their place in the system or, at least, respect for the power of colonial armies.

The maxim of 'born to rule' only works with its corollary of those who are 'born to be ruled'.

And so to the present.

Of the eight top billionaires in the world, three are developers of technology/Internet patents which are used worldwide, one is in telecommunications, three are business magnates and the last is in cosmetics.[205] Their wealth is generated from their global corporations and market investments.

The mantra of economic prosperity, which drives everything, disguises the commercial manipulation at work.

To be clear, **there is nothing wrong with trading** – a fair exchange of goods or money. Trading has been part of world cultures throughout history. Small community businesses are part of the fabric of social interaction. The emphasis should be on **what is fair**.

Indeed, **there is a place for the notion of economic growth** ... at least while it needs to match the growth of population on the planet. However, economic growth can take a range of forms. For example, there is an economic growth which is in balance with fairness, which employs, which does not plunder but recycles, regenerates and disperses its wealth with a moral conscience. That type of growth is not simply driven by profit but by social and environmental factors.

Advocates of the benefits of globalisation acclaim that lots of low-level jobs are being provided in underdeveloped countries to help them in their development. That may be so but **the process can also disguise the agenda of how the very cheap international labour is used** (e.g. as sweat shops, with long hours for minimal pay rates in poor working conditions). Furthermore, that cheap labour is being used to undercut the competitive market and increase a corporation's share of global control – with the bulk of the profits still flowing up the pyramid and increasing the wealth disparity.

The chief executive officers of **global businesses** are on multi-million dollar salaries with performance bonuses built into the package. It is rare for the bonuses not to be paid. It says more about how the packages are presented to the shareholders' meetings than it usually says about corporate performance.

They are doing it because it is legal and … they can. It is also about reinforcing the illusion of wealth as a prime indicator of life's success.

The international companies use **tax havens** in many small countries to minimise the tax that needs to be paid. That process enables profits to be moved and concealed internationally … and for the company to avoid paying the full tax in the country where the profit is made. Meanwhile, the non-global companies in that country still have to pay all their local taxes, without such tax haven advantages – **raising fairness questions**.

The benefits to the global company can involve billions of dollars which would then be used to further amplify the financial success.

The tax havens, themselves, gain by many small donations from the global companies. That can lift a poor country's wealth and allow its people to prosper, **compared to their past**.

The people who actually miss out are those in the countries who generate the initial wealth and whose countries lose the appropriate tax through legal profit shifting.

Other examples include highly paid **sports people** who couldn't receive multi-million dollar salaries on gate receipts alone. Large companies sponsor the personal endorsement arrangements or provide third-party deals with the sports clubs. In August 2017, a Brazilian soccer player was transferred to a French club on a record-breaking deal that will reputedly earn him more **per week** than most elected prime ministers or presidents would earn officially **in a year**.[206] Clearly, companies see a commercial benefit in their brand names being attached to high-profile personalities. It is a marketing approach to inundate media and to retain a corporate association with the fame of desirable success, frequently irrespective of the applicability of their product to the sports person. This is an example of unrestrained market forces. It is legal and it will continue until the mass of the people say, 'Enough!' and demand some checks and balances in the interests of all who live on the planet rather than any particular interest. *That would involve an enormous attitude change. It challenges many current notions of personal freedom, and of personal rights.*

Likewise, the **entertainment industry** has some very highly paid actors, writers and musicians. However, the high advertising profiles of a few conceal the vast number of poorly paid performers who provide the base for those industries' survival. Meanwhile, the studios, recording companies, transport groups and book distribution networks reap very large rewards.

It is marketing – a valid technique for building customer awareness and the cachet of items for trade.

But much of the marketing psychology fuels the mantra of unlimited economic growth.

The 'rightness' of that mantra then permeates society through media advertising, politics, business professional development and university courses.

It becomes an unchallengeable maxim which reinforces the wealth disparity – using the shrugging dismissiveness of 'it is how business works' or 'everybody does it' or 'it has always been like that' or 'you can't change the way the world operates' or 'the market will manage any problems' or 'what can you do?'

Well, small community businesses do not operate the way the corporations do. They are providing a service to their area with an emphasis on sustainability. They pay their taxes, employ local people and are fair with their profit margins. They share their wealth around.

Morality would suggest that trading should be fair or equitable.

But, there is a colonial history of unfair trading ... of making deals which were not fully understood by the weaker parties (e.g. the Rudd concession giving Cecil Rhodes unlimited mining rights in Matabeleland in 1888[207]) or which were made under the duress of intimidation from colonial armies. If gangsters made such deceitful stand-over deals, they would be decried and prosecuted.

Yet, current trading by international conglomerates can also make imbalanced deals with relative impunity.

- The ten richest global corporations (on declared wealth)[208] **each** have more financial resources/assets than most of the world's sovereign countries – most of whom are in debt.[209] Check it out at the URL references supplied in the end notes and with your own research!
- Some of that corporate wealth comes from avoiding paying the usual tax by 'legal' profit shifting to tax havens.[210] Other wealth is generated by using their near market monopoly to legally charge huge profit margins.[211] Check that out as well in the references.

Profit and growth are the main priorities of capitalist economics.

Revisit Christine Lagarde's advice at the start of this chapter. She wanted national policy makers to engage in a granular mix of policies designed to stimulate activity and ensure that the fruits of growth are more evenly spread.

However, corporate wealth can give companies a significant ability to influence government priorities and policies.

How likely is it, then, that the granular mix of policies will be achieved when the global corporations are so financially powerful and operate on a self-centred set of 'profit and growth' priorities?

Clearly, these corporate business tactics do work in terms of profit on the balance sheets and as returns to shareholders. It is what aggressive capitalism is all about. But logic would suggest that it is self-sustaining only as long as there are sufficient, cheap, available inputs and enough buying capacity in the mass of the population.

Trade is good for societies if it is fair – but perhaps not so good if the end result of global corporate control is the wealth disparity shown in the earlier data.

From a moral perspective, where is the long-term benefit to the mass of the world population or the long-term sustainability of the planet?

Are there other solutions? (See Chapter 9)

> *Amass that wealth which has nothing to fear from kings or thieves, and which does not desert thee in the death.*
>
> **The Mahabharata**[212]

Chapter 9

Can philanthropy and self-regulation solve the world wealth imbalance?

Doesn't anyone in power recognise what is happening?

French economist, Thomas Piketty, in his 2014 *Capital in the 21st century*[213] provoked an international debate with a layout of the financial disparity data in the world over the past 250 years. A consensus emerged amongst political and business leaders that the global social and business problems were caused by the **inequality, excessive exclusion** and **distortion associated with modern capitalism.**[214]

At an 'Inclusive Capitalism' conference held in London in 2014,[215] a powerful group including former USA President Clinton, Prince Charles of UK, the Governor of the Bank of England and Christine Lagarde, head of the International Monetary Fund, clearly identified the causes as those listed in bold above and that the present course was unsustainable, **even in economic growth terms.**[216]

Business leaders suggested self-regulating changes to business conduct (such as empowering shareholders in reducing CEO remuneration as well as recognising and containing reckless or unethical behaviour), educational change to equip workforces for the new world and a change in business ownership towards more employee-owned companies.

How much of that self-regulation has happened since 2014?

Does the legality of some of those business processes imply that the process is morally correct?

One might just as well ask if a three-card deception is honest.[217] Both are intended to veil the deceit.

The laws are developed by legislators who often have significant vested interest and benefits (not necessarily illegal) coming their way either in monetary terms or in kind, however disguised. That was the same process which was prevalent during the more overt colonial eras. It is just that the new colonisers are often global corporations.

How much realistic influence do government policy makers have when the international corporations are so powerful in so many ways? The lobbying power of huge conglomerates can be massive.

Should rich people feel guilty about having a lot of wealth?

Several points should be made from a moral standpoint.

- Surely it would depend on how the wealth is acquired.
- If the wealth is acquired by developing activities which provide meaningful work, benefit and livelihoods for many (a social advantage rather than disadvantage), then the process of generating wealth is also a useful community service. That is about sharing wealth in a generic social sense ... and, therefore, more likely to be morally responsible.
- However, if the wealth is achieved by deception in its many forms or by taking advantage of the powerless or by structuring economic activity so that benefits accumulate at the top of the pyramid to the detriment of those at the bottom, then questions could be legitimately asked about the long-term social benefit.

> *That final point is probably the moral key to the process that is presumably responsible for how the disparity in global wealth has come about.*

Some might reasonably argue that whole global economic system has been 'gamed' in favour of those who are already advantaged and that the clever social indoctrination processes, over centuries, have all been designed by the elites to protect the power and prosperity of the *'haves'* from being lost to the *'have nots'*.

Professor Joseph Stiglitz, Nobel Laureate in 2001 in economics, uses his 2012 book, *'The Price of Inequality'*,[218] to explode several of the usual myths such as:

- trickle down economics[219]
- reducing inequality is bad for economic growth
- the top earners made it on their own through their hard work
- the American Dream is about equal opportunities, if not equal outcomes.

Stiglitz claims that many of the unequal outcomes in American society actually depend on the unequal chances given to the young by a parent's occupation. In his view, that is an offshoot of The Matthew Effect,[220] a term coined by Robert Merton in 1968 and named after the Biblical Gospel of Matthew (the parable of talents), where the cumulative effect of capital wealth enables the rich to get richer and the poor to get poorer.

> *Advantage has a way of accumulating. So does disadvantage – thereby compounding the wealth disparity.*

The next moral question might be: how much money does a person need?

When some on the planet survive on a dollar a day, is the saturation coverage of lavish lifestyles the new form of brainwashing the masses into aspiring to some elusive life of wealth?

The ambition is to win a gambling lottery or some other lucky jackpot – which reinforces the desired hope that happiness comes from being wealthy and enjoying an extravagant lifestyle.

Is that a sensible aspiration in a world of such inequality?

Or is it a further marketing ploy to progressively fleece the unwary and sustain the economic status quo? It is the old three-card trick because **gambling ventures** are designed as profit-making businesses. They don't make long-term losses. The occasional jackpot winner is just part of the advertising lure. In addition, they might give gestures of charity back to the community to support children's health activities.

In past eras, the stories were about dreaming to be princes or princesses, or any of the variations of regal power which demanded respect by virtue of their social standing and wealth.

Religions used the awe of their wealth as shown through the power of their symbols – cathedrals, mosques, churches and the paraphernalia of their rituals – to be 'the opiate of the masses';[221] duping the general public into a submissive, calm state.

Wealth can be inherited or earned or both (leaving aside plunder or theft).

> ***Morality is less a function of how much wealth a person has but more about how it is used, in a right way or a wrong way for the benefit of the many.***

That determination would depend on your perspective, your upbringing, your culture and your observation of the world around you.

Does conscience get to some wealthy people?

The old maxim is, 'Money can't buy you love'. There are many examples of what defines wealth or poverty.

For example, over the centuries, the ability to travel at will in order to learn about the world – e.g. the 18th century Grand Tour of Europe[222] – was the privilege of the wealthy. The poor, however, would stay at home in the villages and toil to maintain the economic status quo. Their role was to hear about such adventures, to read the stories and to marvel.

Other measures might include the size of a person's house, or the cars that the successful people drive or the clothes that they wear.

But, in the modern world of mass production, those measures are now available to people in 'the middle class' of the developed and developing world – perhaps part of the benefits of globalisation, perhaps distributed as a salve for the conscience of those who make the decisions.

What about the benefits of philanthropy?

Philanthropy has been part of the culture of many, perhaps most, developed countries. **That is: wealthy people giving back to the community.**

The notion of *noblesse oblige*[223] has been part of the culture of aristocratic families, particularly through the feudal system. There is an obligation on the lord of the manor to look after people who live and work on his property.

Then there are those who made their money through very successful trading ventures or building huge business enterprises, in response to opening up new parts of the world.

For example, **Andrew Carnegie** was a Scottish American who made his money in steel and rail development in the USA in the 19th century.[224] He is often cited as being one of the richest people ever.

In the end, he gave away 90 per cent of his fortune to set up trusts, foundations and universities, to help others.

In 1889, he wrote the article 'The Gospel of Wealth' in which he advocated that the responsibility of the self-made rich was to give back to society.[225]

This was a change from the usual practice of passing huge wealth onto the heirs as an inheritance. Carnegie argued that his approach was the best way to address the wealth inequalities that he observed in his time and he was determined to be remembered for his good deeds rather than his wealth. In time, Carnegie's example has helped to foster a culture of philanthropy in the United States, which continues until this day.

By comparison, **Cecil Rhodes** was a very wealthy 19th century British businessman, mining magnate and politician in South Africa. He developed railways and business endeavours throughout southern Africa. The countries of North and South Rhodesia (now Zambia and Zimbabwe) were named after him. He has scholarships, statues and a university in his name.

However, Rhodes was an avowed imperialist and viewed British Anglo-Saxon stock as the superior race on the planet. He stated in his Last Will and Testament:

'I contend that we are the first race in the world, and that the more of the world we inhabit the better it is for the human race. I contend that every acre added to our territory means the birth of more of the English race who otherwise would not be brought into existence.' [226]

This was a very different motivation from Andrew Carnegie's.

The **United States of America** has had centuries of a culture of social collaboration, built by the early volunteers as a way to not have to rely on an aristocracy for support or a government or a church to solve their public problems.[227] Benjamin Franklin, one of the founding fathers,[228] was regarded in his own time as 'a model of American values' for his **service and generosity to the community**.

In the American Revolution against Britain, the American *continental army* was made up of volunteers. Its commanding general, George Washington, served without pay for three years. He reputedly signed his correspondence at this time, 'Philanthropically yours'.

While the spirit of philanthropy in America dissolved somewhat in the 19th century under the pressure of immigration, industrialisation, urban expansion and a new breed of politicians, Abraham Lincoln's *Gettysburg Address* tried to revive the founding fathers' spirit with:

'Four score and seven years ago our fathers brought forth on this continent, a new nation, conceived in Liberty, and dedicated to the proposition that all men are created equal.'[229]

In modern times, many of the richest Americans such as Mark Zuckerberg and Priscilla Chan,[230] Bill and Melinda Gates,[231] Warren Buffett[232] and Paul Newman[233] have set up their own charitable foundations, particularly to benefit or promote health, equality and education.

Those great acts of generosity are marvellous community gestures. Indeed, these foundations undoubtedly do good work and achieve beneficial outcomes. Some would argue that statues should be, either literally or figuratively, installed as a permanent legacy to the memory of the benefactors.

Others might argue that they are rich people trying to buy virtue, that the scale of donation is less relevant than the motivation behind it.

A man who only has one dollar is giving a huge gesture if he donates 50 cents. Does the man who has many billions, and donates several billions, give with the same motivation? The cynics might add that there is double entry accounting happening – the tax benefit outweighs the outlay. Or that the gesture is more about legacy and to appease a conscience that has far too much wealth.

Americans, along with people in many other developed countries, are very generous in giving to charities. Indiana University research found that 65 per cent of households earning less than $100,000 donated to charity.[234] And most households earning more than that also donated. **There is a social custom of being seen to give to charitable causes.**

However the Washington-based journal, *Chronicle of Philanthropy*, in 2012, published the data that while the poorer families averaged 7.6 per cent of their income in charitable donations, the richer (over $100,000 per year) donated 4.2 per cent of their income.[235]

But …

Perhaps there should be less cynicism about those who choose to give to charity.

After all, the rich person could keep all the wealth and not be a philanthropist at all. As mentioned earlier in this chapter, it would then just pass to the heirs. Surely some gesture of generosity is better than none?

We also shouldn't discount the notions of self-interest and greed in our own lives and attitudes.

Mark Putnam, in his 2003 article, wrote about *'choosing principle over profit'* and highlighted how ingrained in our normal thinking the notion of greed actually is. We often don't realise how self-interested we are. He wrote about how to avoid the temptation to seek much more than you really need and how to stand on principle.[236]

So, does managing one's needs and one's wants become a matter of moral integrity?

Professor Richard Wilkinson of the University of Nottingham[237] has produced a catalogue of statistical correlations (and TED video presentations[238]) that compare indices of social and health problems with the wealth of countries. He found that there was little observable effect when comparing health data against GNI (Gross National Income per head) but he found that:

> ***There are highly significant correlations when comparing social and health problems against wealth inequalities <u>within</u> countries or states.***

That gets away from comparing averages but it looks at the actual range of wealth disparity.[239]

The take-out from his research is that:
- In countries with large wealth disparities, the minority of extraordinary wealthy people have vastly better social and health opportunities than the majority of the poor, average and even well above average, such is the massive range scale of the wealth within those particular countries.
- The second take-out is the implication that a decrease in the wealth disparity within those countries and states should significantly increase the life chances for the majority. The system is not working for the vast majority of people in countries where the range of wealth inequality is largest.

It would be fair to say that Wilkinson's statistical analysis has its critics, particularly that statistics can be expressed in order to support particular agendas or that the indices and definitions of poverty or wealth can be open to interpretation.[240]

Furthermore, the critics point to the possible negative impact of other contributing factors, such as the multi-ethnic make-up of some countries (e.g. USA). They suggest that the countries deemed to be healthier (e.g. Japan, Norway) have an advantage stemming from their more homogeneous ethnic nature.

However, **the critics' rebuttals don't actually debunk the validity of the comparative data**. Perhaps, they also have agendas and are throwing out 'red herring' distracters.[241]

We may now ask the deeper moral question.

Isn't fixing the system, and the culture which promotes it, a better solution than a patchwork of philanthropy and charity?

That will be tackled in the next chapter.

Overcoming poverty is not a task of charity. It is an act of justice.
Nelson Mandela[242]

Chapter 10

Economic growth is the only way forward, even at the expense of using up natural resources. Is that right?

What is the essence of the underlying problem?

Professor Robert Reich of the University of California argued, in 2015, that the current economic model is falling apart.[243] The premises of his argument were:

- *The economic model that dominated most of the twentieth century was mass production by the many, for mass consumption by the many.*
- *Workers were consumers; consumers were workers. As paychecks rose, people had more money to buy all the things they and others produced. That resulted in more jobs and even higher pay.*
- *A future of almost unlimited production by a handful, for consumption by whoever can afford it, is a recipe for economic and social collapse.*
- *The underlying problem won't be the number of jobs. It will be – and it already is – the allocation of income and wealth, which takes away the purchasing power of the majority.*

Reich argued that an economy based on an enormous wealth disparity is a model that can no longer function into the future.

There are other models.

For example, in 2010, Professor Robert Costanza of Vermont University and currently at the Australian National University, proposed a framework for **an ecological economics model**,[244] which, he argued, was both sustainable in terms of its resource use and effectiveness.

Costanza said that:
- conventional economics focuses mainly on the market
- conventional economics does not recognise the externalities that affect the progress of people on the planet
- the planet is finite
- an economy cannot grow indefinitely into this containing system.

His alternative ecological economics model has three interrelated goals of **sustainable scale, fair distribution** and **efficient allocation**. All three of which, he argued, contribute to human well-being and sustainability. He suggests a number of pragmatic mechanisms to change the culture. However, in essence, it means that *'the cut-throat competition is probably going to come to an end, and we'll have more collaboration among the different parts of the system'*.

He also suggests **different measures of success in business.**

We have had triple bottom line accounting for decades, taking into account the social and environmental impacts as well as straight profit. Businesses have learned to ignore the non-profit aspects at their peril in the marketplace. There has been significant cost for transgressors, particularly with some high-profile oil companies whose drills caused substantial leaks.

One example was the BP oil leak in the Caribbean Sea in 2010 which caused half-a-billion dollars loss of earnings in that year and substantial reparations, totalling $61.6 billion, as well as considerable damage to its brand credibility.[245]

Corporate Social Responsibility (CSR) has changed the agenda at the board meetings of large companies in recent decades.[246] Costanza suggests that a **Genuine Progress Indicator** (GPI) could replace Gross Domestic Product (GDP) as a measure that **separates the costs of growth from just the benefits**. That measure has been used in the European Union and in Canada.[247]

If we accept the data from the previous chapters that the global disparity in wealth has reached a critical point, then ...

> ***Morally, we must each look towards correcting the course that the world economies have been on.***

The trajectory dates from the time when the population of the planet was an eighth of its current size and trajectory. That was a time when there was still space for people to relocate.

In addition, **there are sixty-five million people who are either displaced or refugees.**[248] **That is equivalent to nearly the entire population of the United Kingdom** (or close to the population of the states of California and Texas combined) and there are few countries willing to accept more than a few thousand of that number on a permanent settlement basis.

The current economic system is based on capitalism; letting the money flow in free markets on business models which minimise the costs of production and maximise the sales. It is a pyramid structure in which the profits flow largely back to the controllers of the system and the laws of countries have generally been constructed by the beneficiaries of the structure to legalise the process.

Furthermore, the education systems of past centuries, through to the present, have trained the leaders of business (often in selective institutions) in how to view accumulated wealth as the end product of success, no matter how it is obtained. Poverty or social considerations were not options for them. Success was the goal.

Meanwhile, the workers in this economic model were trained to a more functional level (reading, writing and arithmetic) with a strong emphasis on a work ethic (it is a virtue to labour for many hours and many days) and obedience (do what you are told).

The system succeeded as long as the workers believed that the business owners would look after them (*noblesse oblige* – the responsibility of ownership or hereditary title) and while the workers were content with gestures of care (a living wage, two weeks annual holiday, Sundays off and … praise).

The process started to falter when workers organised themselves into trade unions in order to bargain collectively for better working and living conditions and to challenge abuses of power or authority.

More cracks appeared as technology produced increased *automation* – machines could do the tasks of manual labour; robots could carry out sophisticated operations for long hours with minimal human supervision; and computers changed the business practices and banking into an electronic world which needed only a few skilled operatives.

Businesses became very successful, in monetary terms. The investment in technology improved the accounting bottom line because the major cost of wages or salaries was significantly reduced.

However, there was a social cost.

The workers for whom there were no jobs became familiar with the terms *redundant, retrenched, the dole, three-day weeks, casual work, part-time work, functions going off-shore* (to the cheaper labour in developing countries) and the possibility of *retraining*.

From a business viewpoint, there were short-term gains from employing cheap off-shore labour, using automation instead of paying wages, manipulating profits with business costs and, for the largest globalised corporations, to engage sharp accountants to shield their money from scrutiny in low-cost tax havens.

To cap it all, the education systems, research facilities, even the churches (proclaiming the virtues of hard work and obedience) and much of the media endorsed the virtues of the capitalist mindset.

All this was legitimised through the political systems of people who were from the same mindset and social backgrounds as the successful business people.

By the 21st century, masses of people were out of work in many countries, the world resources were being depleted, the media was writing more commonly about climate change and degradation of the natural environment.

Books from the 1960s, which were seen by businesses of the time as scaremongering, now had more resonance. Those were such works as *Silent Spring*[249] by Rachel Carson and *The Population Bomb*[250] by Paul Ehrlich, whose warnings now had decades of research data to support them.

In democracies, the voting public cried, 'Enough of same old, same old'. [251]

'Trickle down economics is not trickling to us'. [252]

They saw the **Global Financial Crisis** of 2008[253] and that the reasons for it stemmed from people who should have been trusted in the banking and financial worlds. They were actually gambling with ordinary people's livelihoods and setting up criminally irresponsible systems which made enormous short-term profits for the already privileged. But those cavalier schemes were doomed to collapse like a tower of playing cards.

From that point on, **politicians' promises** were scrutinised as never before and many were found wanting. Many were charging private business expenses to the tax payers. Some elected representatives, while preaching austerity measures to the general public, set up charades of official electorate business to disguise multiple private trips and exorbitant rorts.²⁵⁴ The hypocrisy significantly reduced their credibility in the eyes of the general public and *'within entitlements'*, *'wouldn't pass the pub test'* or *'snouts in the trough'* became familiar terms in the conventional and social media.

It was as much a reflection on the morality of many parliamentarians as it was about shonky guidelines.²⁵⁵

To illustrate the public disenchantment:
- **'Brexit'**, in 2016, was a public vote, a referendum for a change, from United Kingdom electors.
- The election of the **45th President** of the United States in 2016 was a vote for someone – anyone – in the two-party system, who wasn't part of the old Washington/Wall Street culture.
- The **June 2017 UK general election** was another protest which produced a hung parliament, as the austerity agenda for the masses and the 'old world' wealth disparity emphasised the differences in life opportunities to many in the voting public.

Karl Marx,²⁵⁶ a German philosopher of the 19th century, wrote about the weaknesses of the capitalist model of economic growth. He suggested a more socialist or communist model of **resource sharing and a flattening out of the hierarchical structure of business**.

His arguments have been demonised by many in Western countries, mainly because his system was different from the controlling group's preferred model and a threat to their successful status quo.

They claimed, probably correctly, that Marx's theory would reduce the expected personal freedoms and the unrestrained ability of business to pursue resources for a profit. Shareholders would miss out on dividends and the whole economic structure of the world would be jeopardised.

The word 'communism' became an insidious, almost treasonist, label. Through the McCarthy era in the USA in the 1950s, being branded as a 'communist' was synonymous with the worst kind of enemy.[257]

Throughout the 'Cold War',[258] communism was associated with the Union of Soviet Socialist Republics (USSR) which, as a result of Stalin's[259] reign, had become a despotic and murderous regime, characterised by grey impersonal buildings, people being terrorised by secret police, gulags[260], a low standard of living and … a lack of personal freedoms or the ability to oppose government policies.

The East German (German Democratic Republic) satellite of the Soviet Union was similarly oppressive to its citizens, building the Berlin Wall[261] to prevent escapes to the west. The Stasi (secret police) encouraged people to spy on each other and to report activities to the authorities.

It would have to be conceded that much of that type of the communist experiment was not successful – for a range of reasons but primarily because of corruption and inept, power-craving leadership.

However …

Despots weren't, and aren't, the sole province of communist countries.

There were, and are, many examples of non-communist countries who had dictators ruling with iron fists, not least Nazi Germany, Chile, Argentina and Iraq. Others were ruled under different guises, such as South Africa until 1994 (apartheid regime)[262] or Saudi Arabia (hereditary kingdom), Zimbabwe (military rule, although ostensibly a democracy) and North Korea (military rule, dynastic leadership).

Nevertheless, while Karl Marx's philosophical ideas of a different way have been shunned by Western political and economic thinkers, **many successful Western businesses actually have flattened their**

management structures in the manner that Marx described and had more sharing of the financial success.[263]

Likewise, the 'communist' **People's Republic of China** should be given credit for significantly reducing the fertility rate of its huge population and getting 500 million people out of extreme poverty.[264] The modern success of communist China is frequently criticised because of its record on human rights and because it doesn't think like the Western model of capitalism or governance. But its growing prosperous middle class of China is fast challenging the USA on its economic success.

In the 1950s and 60s, communist **North Vietnam** gave the powerful French military, and then the very powerful US military/political leadership, a bloody nose during two decades of war in North and South Vietnam.

While losing many hard-fought battles to armies with superior resources, the North Vietnamese kept bouncing back. As a people, they were prepared to sacrifice many more lives than their enemy in a bid to wear down the aggressors in the arena of political and public opinion, and to rid themselves of colonial or invading powers.

Despite many individual regular and conscripted soldiers serving the political decisions of their respective countries with honour and noble motives, at the micro level there were atrocities, as in many wars. Some of those[265] plus the general impacts of war on combatants and civilians were televised worldwide to a general public who were not used to seeing the violent reality of armed combat on television in their lounge rooms – rather than the movie versions or censored newsreels.

World opinion was swayed.

The infallibility and disingenuous geo-political statements of world leaders with powerful armies were challenged by vocal populations.

In the end, the US troops and their allies were withdrawn in a face-saving peace deal.

In the aftermath in Vietnam, there was a significant crackdown on personal freedoms of the general population by the victorious North, including sentencing many of the South Vietnamese population to 're-education' camps. That didn't endear communism to the Western-aligned countries who had been fighting for years to assist those people in the south.

Decades later, however, the doomsday predictions of the communist domino effect have not happened.

Vietnam is today a thriving country with a mixture of operating principles.

The Marxist ideas of **flattening the wealth disparity** should not be disregarded out of hand just because of past conflicts or that Stalin's despotic USSR was not a success or that the communist Chinese and Russians supported the North Vietnamese.

Likewise, **communism, as we have known it, should not be touted as the answer.** Some of the principles could prove to be useful but the 20th century communist interpretations of Marx's ideas were hi-jacked by authoritarian regimes ... and they largely failed their founding philosopher's ideals.

It should also be noted that there are many failures within Western democracies as well, as the wealth disparity and disenchantment in the electorates can attest.

This is not an argument against capitalism –
as in fair trading,
but
it is an argument against the <u>unchecked capitalism</u> which has created the wealth disparity and the attitudes which support it.

Societies throughout history have had **checks and balances** to try to ensure that immoral commercial and political behaviour is minimised. These are examples such as the separation of powers, government regulation and laws against anti-social behaviour.

Major checks against corporate excess are:

- **The voting power of shareholders.** However, shareholders are investors who have a strong interest in share-value increase and a strong dividend return.
- **Government fair trading regulation.** While there are agencies to monitor and prosecute improper collusion or monopoly power, they operate within the parameters of the laws of the land – which, in turn, are subject to the lobbying influence of powerful political forces.
- **International governmental co-operation** to identify, control and prosecute such activities as profit shifting to avoid tax. This is subject to similar lobbying power.
- **Corporate self-regulation.** While this would be an ideal, it needs an independence of monitoring with collective consequences for any who misuse their power.
- **The voting power of the people.** There are significant recent indicators that populations are voting for change, for no more of the old policies and for fairness, in having meaningful work to support families and communities.

Capitalism has a place in future modelling ... if by capitalism, we mean the fair trading ethics that are exemplified by most small community businesses, that employ local people, treat employees with dignity and share the wealth with society, not just investors.

Changing the economic model isn't a choice between capitalism and something else, such as communism. That would just be compounding the errors of history. It is about realising that all models have flaws and advantages and it doesn't have to be a one-size-fits-all.

The last thing the world needs is to get stuck in another either/or fallacy.

By the time, you have read all of these twenty one chapters, an approach to a possible answer should become obvious to you.

From a moral point of view, perhaps ego and self-righteousness get in the way of a rational examination of perspectives.

So we can now ask:

Is there a way forward for a model of economics which doesn't rely on infinite growth on a finite planet?

Harrison Ford, the American actor, made a profound statement on a 2016 visit to Australia:

'Nature will take care of itself – nature doesn't need people, people need nature to survive. The planet will be OK, there just won't be any damn people on it.' [266]

Sir David Attenborough, in an address to the Royal Geographic Society in 2013, said:[267]

'I have little doubt that if we have the capacity to limit our birth rate, then we should consider doing that. We have a finite environment – the planet. Anyone who thinks that you can have infinite growth in a finite environment is either a madman or an economist.'

As suggested in this chapter, more and more of **the voting public are becoming educated and active** about:

- reining in the unrestricted digging up of finite resources (fuels and minerals)
- objecting to transforming the natural environment (such as cutting pristine forests, using prime agricultural land for urban growth or fracking[268])
- blocking the release of gases into the atmosphere (causing polluting smogs in many major cities as well as probably helping to warm the Earth and melt large ice sheets[269]).

There are studies which suggest the viability of renewable energy resources[270] (such as hydro, thermal, solar, tidal, wind) or recycling (paper, plastic, glass, metal, technology hardware) or the powering of vehicles by electricity from non-polluting sources.

Transition to renewable industries can be delivered in stages. It doesn't have to be all or nothing. That is a polarising fallacy.

There is a source of employment in these renewable industries. The research and development has been slow to some extent because of the influence of vested interests in the current economic model.

It is much like the development of hybrid and electric cars which was stymied by the car making companies who were making large profits with petrol and diesel vehicles.[271]

The message is that many profitable businesses like to monopolise the market and enjoy the *status quo*. Their political and financial acolytes are mainly from the same schools of thought, perhaps even the same actual educational institutions.

Change tends to happen in the market economies, only when it is forced upon them.

The rise in oil prices has done just that to the American culture of gas-guzzling cars. Meanwhile, the Asian car companies have automated the production of low-emission cars. They have left the US car companies in their wake … to examine the merits of their stationary economic model.

With these illustrations of a shaky future for the current economic models, there might be a realisation that things are now at a tipping point.

What is the moral choice?

Former Australia prime minister and treasurer, Paul Keating said in a 2004 address:[272]

A Philosophical Morality Challenge

'Leadership is about interpreting the future to the present; having the ability to see over the horizon; letting those wider coordinates inform one's thinking ... In a world constantly changing under influences like globalisation and rapid communications, the premium has to be on quantum changes ... The new world belongs to paradigm shifts in thinking and flexibility in management.'

But there are strong interests and lobby groups who will stay with the current system as long as the profit continues to be made.

Furthermore, in most democratic countries, politicians are elected for short terms in office. Election campaigns in the modern era are very expensive, due to travel costs and advertising expectations across a range of media.

Donations to the political parties are matters of significant influence. (See earlier evidence of the wealth of global corporations.)

Politicians are subject not only to the wishes of the people who elected them but also to the pragmatism of party structures and the wishes of powerful people in the shadows.

Essentially, **modern politicians are risk averse.** They don't want to take the chance on not being re-elected – which seems to be a major priority – or on taking the quantum leaps that Paul Keating advocated.

So, is the moral choice to take the strategic view, a longer term perspective?

Yes. The evidence would suggest that it could be about the survival of the planet or, at least, the ways of living on Earth.

Is it possible to get beyond trying to find new iterations of old colonial economic theories? Or **is our thinking trapped by our social and academic conditioning?**

> *If your only tool is a hammer, then every problem looks like a nail.*[273]

Can our best brains focus on more sustainable models, even if that might bring some restriction on business rights? For example, do we need to keep using up natural resources in preference to developing recyclable or sustainable options – just because it is easier and less expensive in the short term ... and because we can?

Philosopher and writer, Iris Murdoch (1919–1999), suggests that the moral decisions, you might make, will be determined by your upbringing to this point.[274] And, across the globe, we come from many different cultures and upbringings.

Can there be common ground on some strategic aspects without degenerating into the stalemate of oppositional poses?

It is a very important moral and strategic question.

Even after the destruction and viciousness of great wars in recent history (post World War II), the majority of resolutions (after Korea, Vietnam, Afghanistan, Iraq and Syria) have involved – and still involve – the antagonists sitting down and negotiating a way forward.

Can the same happen with the economic challenges, without us all having to suffer the pain of disasters or wars first?

> *Anyone who thinks that you can have infinite growth in a finite environment is either a madman or an economist.*
>
> **Sir David Attenborough**

Chapter 11

Is it human nature to put people into 'boxes', categories – he/she is 'that type of person'?

Is your self esteem based on someone else's opinion of you ... or whatever box others might fit you into?

When you meet new people, don't you immediately start to form impressions just from their appearance and their manner?

Male/female, well groomed, fashion sense, carrying themselves with confidence, jewellery, wedding rings, look you in the eye, handshake ...

Do they look like you? Is there a smile?

Then, beyond the pleasantries, the questions start:

What is your name? Is that an accent? Where do you work? Where do you live? Do you follow sport? What about the arts? Favourite movie? What writers do you like? Do you travel a lot? Where are you planning to go next? What do you like most about living here?

These are examples of social niceties used in many cultures to engage a person in polite casual conversation. But they are also a means of categorising a person as: a pleasant person, a potential friend, a useful business connection ... or alternatively, someone who you don't like, someone to avoid, someone who is different, someone down on their luck, someone not to cross …

So, is it human nature to classify things or people?
In 2010, Harvard University psychologist Professor Alfonso Caramazza found, in studies of sighted and blind people, that the brain makes associations of danger in two separate areas of the visual cortex, whether or not the object has ever been sighted.[275] It is a neural process of classification into threat or no threat, irrespective of seeing the scenario.

Princeton University cognitive neuroscientist, Marius Peelen, who was not involved in Caramazza's research, suggests that the finding shows that visual recognition is not needed to activate those separate areas of the brain and that perhaps the wiring is an innate response to any sense of potential danger.[276]

An implication of such studies is that the brain is hardwired to classify things or people into different categories … and that it could happen automatically.

We are back to that nature versus nurture discussion.

If we accept some innate categorising function in our brains, are we also socialised into putting people into 'boxes'?
Socialisation is how we learn the norms and beliefs of our particular society. From our earliest family and play experiences, we are made aware of societal values and expectations. Classifying people is part of that process – who they are: family, friend, someone we visit, stranger.

The influence of family, schooling systems, peer groups and the laws of the land tell a person how to fit into a culture and how to identify others who may come from the same or different backgrounds.[277] It is the overt, as well as the often hidden, curriculum for learning about belonging. There are nuances of attitudes that we absorb just by living in a particular social setting; listening to elders and peers; reading social and mainstream media.

Businesses often put prospective employees through a range of selection tests, such as for personality characteristics (e.g. Myers-Briggs[278]). Others use tests of emotional intelligence.[279] They are all designed to fit people into types to suit the business's agenda or people that might need particular understanding or care, if employed.

Employment opportunities in Western democracies usually require transparent, equitable, recruitment processes, although the presence of covert selection indicators of social connection should not be discounted (e.g. which school or university you attended or where you live or even what you have written on social media). It is the farming notion of coming from 'good stock' or 'good breeding'; being of a quality and fit to belong to the organisation.

So, if someone is deeply socialised into particular values, beliefs and ways of operating, then a change to anything new can be quite a scary phenomenon.

It is not always easy to be asked to 'walk in someone else's shoes', to see the world from a different perspective, to accept someone who speaks a different language or who comes as a refugee from a land that operates differently, with different nurturing styles.

Unless a person's upbringing has prepared him/her for accepting a range of differences, it can cause a shying away from the uncomfortable, from the unfamiliar. To adapt one's thinking to accommodate such newcomers can mean a major process of re-socialisation.

Or, alternatively, it can create a xenophobic reaction of not wanting to be involved with change; not wishing to put in the effort to deal with people who have that sense of 'otherness' – something to be feared or rejected.

It canvasses ideas of belonging and of worth – from the basic notion that what our family and society have taught us must be right. That can instil a peculiar nationalistic arrogance which sees others either as a threat or as lesser people.

If we accept the samples of research indicated earlier, then there might be an innate wiring to recognise threats (a fight or flight response) which is tailored further by the society of our upbringing to be accepting/accommodating or resisting.

Given that none of us had a choice in where we were born or to whom, nor to the society which has influenced our upbringing, then where does the moral choice come in, for us in later life?

Perhaps, into the future, it could be in the learning of critical-thinking techniques to recognise the socialisation process for what it is, to question it, to seek evidence for moral challenges and to find solutions.

The practices of cults form one illustration of a methodology that tries to influence the thinking of its members to be non-critical and accepting of whatever doctrine is being promoted.[280] It is similar in some ways to the education and re-education programs used in many cultures. See what you think.

These are such techniques as:
- ensuring that you regularly attend training in the expected behaviours;
- offering impressive buildings, uniforms or the trappings of power to act as a valued inspiration for your aspiration to be part of the group;
- having a hierarchy of leadership/status into which you can be inducted progressively as a reward and to show that you are learning to be obedient.

There are often charismatic leaders who have the ability to persuade by their words, their command of ideas, their ability to synthesise the complex world into simple mantras.

- They might also use trance-inducing rituals of collective team familiarity such as singing or chanting together or holding hands as a group. That can bring on a sense of inner peace.
- Likewise, parading in step … or listening, as part of a congregation, to hypnotic chants provide the simple comfort of placing yourself in the hands of leaders who can make decisions for you.
- Repetitive acknowledgement of acceptable behaviours is a strong socialisation feature while there are unpleasant consequences for deviation from the norm. That can lead to isolating and decrying you if you don't follow the expected pathway.

The regular training sessions emphasise that:
- your self-worth is based on your belonging to the group and that outsiders have less or no worth.

Your leaders might:
- mesmerise and guilt-trip you so that you don't deviate from the path or challenge the version of truth that you are hearing.
- encourage you to reveal your innermost fears, doubts and past misdeeds to unburden your conscience, while that information can also later be used to control or shame you.
- ask you to commit money so that you are financially compromised.
- require you, more and more, to socialise only with like-minded people and to view outsiders, who might have alternative views, as unacceptable companions.

The wave of indoctrination is all that you are allowed to hear so that your mind gradually accepts that it must be right.

Finally, you might be asked to recruit others into the group so that they can go through the same mind-altering process.

At first read, **that example might appear to be a fairly extreme process of socialisation.** Think of your own life journey. Are there any similarities in how you learned your culture?

Many respected social institutions (e.g. religions or schools) may well use one or two of these techniques to educate or re-educate. **Only oppressive mind-controllers would use them all.**

There is a significant difference between a cult and many religions.

To illustrate, let us respectfully leave aside the individual's personal beliefs in deities or in supernatural occurrences or the ability of religions to influence people's thinking.

Socially, many religions have genuine gestures of welcoming; of sharing with others in the community especially through a calendar of celebratory events (e.g. Christmas, Ramadan). Many demonstrate a sense of goodwill towards others beyond their religion; of bringing comfort and of supporting people through the hardships of life such as illness, homelessness or bereavement. In essence, their gestures of help transcend whatever 'box' the recipient might be categorised as being in.

That is a very different approach from the excluding nature of cults which seek to isolate their members from the 'corrupting influence' of outsiders.

Contrast the cult process with someone who is taught:
- to read widely, perhaps in more than one language
- to listen to lots of differing viewpoints without making initial judgements
- to seek out evidence from multiple frames of reference, before forming an opinion.

In that second case, the person might be asked to question, to imagine and to research what it might be like to live like someone else, like 'the outsider', the person who is different or living another lifestyle – and not just the prince or princess style of the fairy tales.

What might it be like:
- **not** to have won the lottery of life, **not** to have been born with great advantages, not being able to read?
- to be criticised for things that you can't change, such as where you were born or your appearance or your accent?
- for someone, who is denied access to schooling, to plead for a chance to get an education or to learn a language other than the first language or to get a range of answers to questions about life or to be able hear different viewpoints?
- for someone born poor, or trapped in economic slavery, to get a chance for a free job prospect?
- for a starving person to eat and then to be able to get satisfying work in order to feed his/her family?

The person in this second example is not being indoctrinated (or brainwashed) into a single 'right way' of thinking.

He/she:
- is learning to identify with others in different situations, to see many different ways forward – **to empathise**.
- is practising the power of logical thinking – to ask questions, to seek out the consequences of actions, including the unintended ones.
- can look at another person and not automatically fit him or her into a particular labelled box.

There is an ability to, perhaps, see potential rather than just 'otherness', to see someone to learn alongside or with or from, rather than to make superior or inferior opinions.

He/she can read situations or listen to opinions with a critical mind … and then make choices based on evidence.

*Morally, whether or not it is innate human nature to classify others, making judgements about others should be based on **what behaviour and personality is demonstrated rather than some predetermined filter of acceptance familiarity or the wariness of difference.***

The skill of the critical thinker is to recognise the social categorisation process for what it is and to retain an open mind when meeting others.

Got any dirt between your toes from walking on my land?
Aboriginal wisdom

Chapter 12

Does context affect human rights?

Not all countries accept the principles of the Universal Declaration of Human Rights.

The 1948 Universal Declaration of Human Rights (UDHR) has been endorsed by convention in many Western countries.[281] It takes its historical and philosophical roots from the debates in the age of the Enlightenment.

Forty-eight countries signed the original UDHR in 1948, albeit that many African countries were excluded through being colonies or dependencies of colonial powers. The allowable members of the United Nations who voted against the UDHR were Saudi Arabia, USSR, Belorussia, South Africa, Ukraine, Poland and Czechoslovakia. Many more countries, since 1948, have affiliated in principle or have become signatories of the UDHR.

However, **the Declaration of Cairo in 1990 laid out a different philosophy** as interpreted mainly by Muslim countries. That Cairo Declaration has been signed by forty-five countries. It guarantees many of the same rights as the UDHR, while at the same time reaffirming the inequalities which are inherent in Islamic law. **Their world view is different.**[282]

THE MOST AVOIDED QUESTIONS

Does that make it wrong?

Is the moral test one of context?

Do these perceived inequalities stand the test of logical reasoning?

The traditions of the Islamic religion, which govern the countries that are signatories to Cairo Declaration, see as normal such priorities as:

- religious conversion to their particular religion
- different rules for men and women, particularly with respect to marriage and political freedoms.

Before people in the Western democracies adopt a 'holier than thou' position:

- Religious conversion has been a priority in religions such as Judaism and Catholicism for centuries.
- Christian missionaries have used it as their *raison d'être* throughout past centuries – to convert people to their interpretation of Christianity.

Likewise, giving women access to political rights in the Western cultures has been a feature only of the last ten decades. Indeed, it is only in relatively recent times that such matters as equality in marriage, in employment and in the social leadership have been the subjects of debates and reluctant concessions in the Western religions and societies.

The Islamic view of women in marriage is one of the complementarity of functions, rather than equality – emphasising the distinction between femininity and masculinity. **That is a different view from the current Western ideas, but not necessarily very different from recent historical Western practices where women had a primarily child-rearing function.**

Traditionally, Islamic marriage has also been associated with making alliances between families. That is also certainly not unknown in Western countries either (cf. the marriages of British Queen

Victoria's nine children into the aristocratic families of Europe and Russia.[283])

Like her male counterpart in Islamic society, each woman is under a moral and religious obligation to seek knowledge, to develop her intellect, to broaden her outlook, to cultivate her talents and then to utilise her potential for the benefit of her soul and her society.[284]

There are many examples – both in the early history of Islam and in the contemporary world – of Muslim women who have played prominent roles in public life, including being sultanas, queens, elected heads of state[285] and successful businesswomen. It also important to recognise that, in Islam, home and family are firmly situated at the centre of life: a man's work cannot take precedence over the private realm.[286]

Are there tangible measures of human rights?

If people are to have a choice to move beyond a single view of the world, **the ability and opportunity to read** might be a useful indicator.

Notwithstanding these priorities for women outlined in the Qu'ran, UNICEF (United Nations International Children's Emergency Fund) in 2007 noted that out of twenty-four nations with less than 60 per cent female primary school enrolment rates, seventeen were Muslim nations.

In several of those Muslim countries, more than half the adult population was functionally illiterate and the proportion reached 70 per cent among Muslim women.[287]

- In 2012, UNESCO (United Nations Educational, Scientific and Cultural Organisation) estimated that the literacy rate among adult women was about 50 per cent or less in a number of Muslim-majority countries, including Morocco, Yemen, Bangladesh, Pakistan, Niger, Mali, Gambia, Guinea, Guinea-Bissau, and Chad.[288]

- Egypt had a women's literacy rate of 64 per cent in 2010. Iraq had 71 per cent and Indonesia had 90 per cent.
- While literacy has been improving in Saudi Arabia since the 1970s, the overall female literacy rate in 2005 was still only 50 per cent, compared to male literacy of 72 per cent.[289]

At a global level, literacy amongst 15–24 year olds, according to UNICEF in 2016, had increased to around 91 per cent and it was about the same for both genders **in two-thirds of the countries that they measured.** However, the gender imbalance still exists in the other third. It is most pronounced in Saharan Africa, Afghanistan, Pakistan and India where young women account for 59 per cent of the illiteracy.[290]

Clearly, **the literacy practices in certain Muslim countries are different from the expectations of many Western countries** – but …

Even in the developed countries, there is a difference in the reality between intended and actual outcomes.

For example:
- The literacy rate in 2013 for the **United States** was declared at 86 per cent but, within that statistic, **only 43 per cent of adults were able to read to 5th grade level.**[291] According to the US National Assessment of Adult Literacy, there had been no improvement over the previous ten years.
- Likewise, 70 per cent of inmates in America's prisons cannot read above Grade 4 level.[292]

There is no moral high ground there.

Let us return to the declarations of human rights, where we clearly have two world views depending on the context of their national governance systems.

The divergence, at least superficially, seems to come from a strong dependency on religious interpretation for their legal systems in the

Cairo Declaration compared to a more liberal approach to legislation in the Western democracies who have signed up to the UDHR.

Another measure of human rights in a country is the incarceration of its people.

- The top five countries for imprisonment in the world in 2016 were the USA (at 2,193,798 prisoners), China (at 1,548,498), then the Russian Federation, Brazil and India.[293] So much for the United States of America as 'the land of the free'.
- Even if we look at the incarceration rates per 100,000 in the population, the USA (total population of 356 million) still ranks second behind the tiny Seychelles (total population of ninety thousand), who, for example, have imprisoned over 100 Somali pirates in the past three years.[294]

These are a couple of examples (amongst many indicators) of context and the rights of individuals. It should be clear that the interpretation of human rights varies considerably across the planet.

What should the moral position be?

Won't it depend on your perspective and your ability to make changes in the governance systems of your nations?

Where there is a restriction on protests, backed up by harsh judicial punishments for transgression, your view might well express the frustrations or acceptance of your context?

By contrast, if you are in a position of power in a dictatorial regime, perhaps your perspective of life chances might encourage you to retain the status quo with whatever justification that you might choose.

Is there a correct stance on human rights?
Correctness might well be a relative term.
It could depend on perspective – the rulers, the masses, the level of belief as compared to critical thinking.

Certainly, history would suggest some occasions when **the power of the people has overcome the absolute nature of a ruler** or rulers in order to establish the human rights of the masses.

- **Charles I** was executed in 1649 CE when he claimed the divine right of kings to rule and the English Civil War deposed him.[295]
- Earlier, in 1215 CE, a revolt of the barons in England forced John I to sign the **Magna Carta,** guaranteeing certain human rights before the law.[296] The interpretations of that document are still used today within the US Supreme Court to justify certain rights.
- In 1775–1783 CE, the **American War of Independence** was an expression of people power in the Thirteen Colonies to rid themselves of the rule of George III of Britain.[297]
- The subsequent **American Civil War** in 1861–1865 CE was a conflict between the Unionists in the North, who were opposed to the slavery in the South and to the economic model which relied upon it. The conflict came to a head when the Confederates of the southern states wanted to secede from the Union and continue their slave practice. The North went to war with the South to settle the moral question.[298] The North won … at significant human cost.
- In the 1788–1799 CE **French Revolution,** the aristocracy was overthrown by the people and King Louis XVI of France was executed by the revolutionaries in a successful attempt to stop the absolute power of the monarchy.[299]
- In 1917 CE, the **Russian Revolution** deposed centuries of Tsarist autocracy in Russia.[300] As with many revolutions, the country descended into a five-year civil war as the opposing ideologies fought for power.
- More recently, in 1947 CE, the **Chinese Revolution** changed the country from a land of dynastic emperors to the modern day People's Republic of China. There are many queries about the record of Chinese human rights as

a communist republic and where morality should lie in the face of trying to manage a 1.4 billion population.

To balance the record of history, there are also many examples of potential revolutions that were trying to assert the human rights of the disadvantaged who were, in some cases, the majority. But they were crushed by powerful armies.

- In 72–71 BCE, **Spartacus** led a slave rebellion, fighting for freedom against the oligarchy of the Roman Empire. The valiant resistance was overcome by the power of the eight legions of Marcus Crassus and the 6,000 survivors of the revolt were reportedly crucified along the Appian Way leading into Rome – as an example to others.
- In 1533–1544 CE, **Manco** – the puppet Inca leader – escaped from the abuses of Spanish rule in 1536 and led a nine-year rebellion against his conquerors. He claimed the lives of his old foes, Francisco Pizzaro and Diego del Almagro. But, in the end, Manco was assassinated, his followers were dispersed and the Spanish rule continued until 1572.[301]
- The **Indian Revolution** of 1857–1859 CE was a rebellion against the British East India Company in the upper Ganges valley. It was a reaction to a catalogue of religious insensitivities as well as the domineering brutal attitude of a colonial power. After 2,392 British men, women and children were reportedly killed by rebels in the revolts,[302] the British army prevailed and 100,000 Indians died in the wars.[303]

The catalogue of failed defiance is long.

There is the resistance of the **North American Indians** to European settlement. The same is true with **Aboriginal Australians** against the waves of European immigrants. In the 1980s and 90s, the attempts at regime change in **Iraq** and **Libya** resulted in horrendous reprisals against the rebels – until both dictators were eventually removed decades later. It is debatable, even now, how much improvement in human rights has been made in these countries.

Likewise, in 2017, the **Syrian Army**, assisted by the Russians, appears to have largely overcome a collection of rebel groups that were trying to overthrow the documented atrocities of the Assad regime.[304]

At present, in **Africa** and **Asia** there are a number of totalitarian dictatorships. They are backed up by insuperable military power, plus sophisticated indoctrination regimes.

The correctness of the stance on human rights in these cases has proved to have less impact than the controlling interpretation of those who have stronger military forces.

Does context influence what is accepted as right?

Surely, what you will accept as *right* will depend on the circumstances that you live under, how particular attitudes have been inculcated from your earliest years, how easily you can access multiple sources of information, your ability to critically assess that information … and whether you will live or die.

An eye for an eye will only make the whole world blind
Mahatma Ghandi

Chapter 13

Fallacies or fact. Are media factoids being believed?

We live in a world of information.

We are inundated with a range of media, including advertisers encouraging us to be involved in a host of great new things. Corporate entities and ideologues use the authority of bewildering science or statistics to justify the beneficial qualities of whatever they wish to sell or promote.

In an earlier age, newspaper reports were generally accepted as a trusted source of information; however, now it is hard to distinguish between straight factual reporting and opinion.

It is tabloid!

Snobbery denigrates some sources in favour of others. So 'tabloid' – which once referred to the size of the page in a newspaper – is now used to belittle the contribution of certain newspapers or television reports as light-weight reporting, fake news or sensation. *'It is tabloid'* can now be a derogatory term, suggesting poor quality fiction passing itself off as reality or news.[305]

The same process is sometimes in play with the term, 'social media' – using the example of some poor quality posts and trolls to imply that all social media is false, light-weight, unsubstantiated opinion and should be disregarded.

Television panel discussions have supposed authorities pronouncing and extrapolating, based on their opinions or data from opinion polls of dubious accuracy bases.

A typical classic question is of the style: 'I know you were not in the room but what do you think they were saying?' The subsequent discussion of opinion, dressed up as implied fact, can then continue for minutes. It is a parallel world of supposed facts.

No doubt, some viewers would take such commentary as being well-informed, just as others might take the outlandish statements made in political campaigns as being correct predictions of future behaviour. Or they might read clearly false information as fact ... because they want to believe that it is true. That is known as *confirmation bias*.[306]

Let us dissect this a little.

A fact is a generally accepted truth which can be verified by experiment and testing from a range of sources.[307]

Note: It will not have escaped the astute reader that this writer uses a range of references in this book to question moral standpoints. Their use does not imply that they must be facts, merely that those referenced opinions or data are freely available to support particular arguments.

A **factoid** is a known falsehood[308] which is presented as truth and repeated until, as an *availability heuristic*,[309] it is accepted by many that it must be true.

A **fallacy** is a mistaken belief, particularly based on unsound arguments.[310]

In addition, the ability of social media platforms to track the personal habits of participants creates the opportunity for targeted advertising and also for enabling **the feed of misinformation** which might confirm readers' views of the world.

For example, in December 2016, a man fired shots in a Washington pizza parlour, based on his belief that a fictitious social media story was true. The man told the police that he'd come to the restaurant to self-investigate an offensive conspiracy theory that had spread online during the presidential candidate Hillary Clinton's run for the White House.[311]

We are currently in the age of **alternative facts** or alternative truths, made popular by the spokespeople for the 45th President of the United States of America.[312] These are bold statements – some of which are certainly incorrect – delivered for effect and to distract from other issues, particularly through the media (mainstream and social).

The President himself also makes statements of dubious factual accuracy, to imply some deeper meaning, about which the American electorate should be worried.

For example, in the President's first address to Congress on 28 February 2017, he announced, *'We are also taking strong measures to protect our nation from radical Islamic terrorism'* [313] – a statement which followed his earlier campaign jibes of *'We now have an administration and a former secretary of state who refuse to say* radical Islamic terrorism.' [314] He then issued an executive order, #13769, to ban travel to the USA from several primarily Muslim countries.[315]

While it is acknowledged that there have been many media headlines which have attributed acts of terror to Islam, *the availability heuristic,*

> **the implication was that he, the President, had identified the major incoming threats of terrorism to the USA and that he derided people who would not even name that terrorism for what he says it is.**

However ...

Journalist, David Neiwert,[316] analysed and detailed 201 terrorism incidents that had occurred in the USA from 2008 to 2016. (Neiwart was based at the Centre for Investigative Reporting[317] – a non-profit media centre in California.) He found only 1 per cent of perpetrators or alleged perpetrators of terrorism were from countries listed in the President's travel ban. An overwhelming 87 per cent of them were US-born.[318]

The policy message, which the President is entitled to deliver, might well refer to radicalising messages delivered over the Internet; however, it does not tally with the evidence of terrorists physically entering the country. **That information is given to sell an idea to the American public.**

How do you present fallacies as persuasive arguments?

Let us consider some of the techniques that are used in so many walks of life to use fallacies to persuade.[319] They are not new to this era.

Some of them are based on unacceptable premises, such as:

- *You can't prove that it is not true so don't criticise me for believing that it is true.* This is used in many discussions about religion or belief, which is a shift in the burden of proof from evidence to lack of evidence. A similar technique is also known as **the appeal to ignorance** (*argumentum ad ignorantium*). *No-one has proved the claim false therefore it must be true.* Such as, no-one has proved that there is no life on Mars or Jupiter. Therefore, there is life on these planets. It is an illogical extrapolation.
- The **Sorites paradox** is where the arguer claims that we can't identify the point on a continuum where a grain of sand becomes a heap of sand.[320] This is used regularly in 'the right-to-life' discussions. *When does an embryo become*

a person? You can't define that precisely. Therefore, it is argued, there is no moral difference between an embryo and a baby at birth.
- The **slippery slope** fallacies. Don't take the innocent first step because it will be impossible not to take the next, and the next ... So, don't get a credit card or you will be 'maxed out' in debt, which will lead to gambling and then to stealing and a life of crime. It takes no account of the self-control which many people demonstrate daily. The same argument is often used in debates about changing the laws on assisted suicide for people who have painful terminal illnesses and are seeking legal permission to choose the right to die. The slippery slope argument has old people being killed without their consent. This ignores the factual evidence to the contrary from countries and states whose laws currently allow assisted suicide.[321]
- The **faulty analogy**. My last three cars were reliable and they were all red. So, I will buy a red car.
- The **hasty generalisation**. The oldest woman in the world smoked most of her life until the age of 117, therefore smoking is not bad for you.[322] The sample might be a little small and definitely not random.
- The **strawman** uses a distortion or caricature in an opponent's argument to then attack the weakened part of the argument, not the real one. That is simplistic popular distraction which doesn't solve the actual problem. For example, reduce carbon dioxide and we will have less greenhouse gases, thereby helping to reduce the effects of climate change. Cars produce carbon dioxide so we will ban cars. Or, some terrorists were descended from refugees. So, we will ban all future refugees. Or, some terrorists claim to be influenced by a religious tradition. So, we will ban any religion that the terrorists claimed and that isn't ours.
- The **'ad hominen'** technique attacks the person rather than the argument. *What could he know about economics, he's a biologist?*

- The fallacious **appeal to authority**. *I tell you he is a fine man and a noble man* does not necessarily qualify him to talk on women's rights, for example, unless he is specifically qualified in that area. Or the news presenter or sports person does not equate to being a well-informed authority on everything. Brand endorsement should be within the level of expertise.
- The **fallacy of ambiguity** or **false dichotomy**. This is a favourite of politicians. *You are either for this or against it* assumes that only two positions are possible. Indeed, the positions could both be wrong and there could be many other possibilities.
- The **fallacy of composition**. Men are on average taller than women, therefore Bob must be taller than Alice. But Alice is 185 cm and Bob is 173 cms.
- The **appeal to popularity**. Hundreds of people or thousands of people can't be wrong. History would suggest otherwise on a range of strongly held views (e.g. the Earth is flat).
- The **appeal to tradition**. It has been done like this for centuries. That can't be wrong. But times and contexts can change (e.g. motor cars have replaced horse-drawn carriages).
- The **appeal to pity or affection**. This is well known to parents. *If you really loved me, you would get me a puppy.*

The list of potential fallacy techniques is much longer than these examples, as my earlier reference source suggests.

In essence, the persuader is using:

- **confirmation bias** (relying on your experience and saying things that you might want to hear, whether they are true or not)
- **heuristics** (mental shortcuts, whereby if something is repeated often enough in the media you will come to accept it as fact because you have heard it said often – not whether the real data supports the assertion, e.g. the growth in number of terrorist attacks)

- **question framing** (*if we do this, then 50 per cent of the people will live* sounds better than saying that *if we do this, 50 per cent of the people will die*) or using one or more of the many types of fallacies (see above)
- simply **telling bald lies with confidence,** in the hope that no-one will check (alternative truths).[323]

So, are media factoids being believed?

Journalist, Roy Greenslade, in his *Guardian* article of 2016,[324] asks, *'Is truth relevant any longer? Journalists are encouraged to accept the philosophy behind the adage famously coined by* The Guardian's *CP Scott:* **Comments are free but facts are sacred.'**

Greenslade argues that the truth often turns out to be a moving target. It is influenced by political, economic and social decisions, twisted as propaganda tools to suit the required narrative argument. He suggests that when CP Scott wrote his *facts-are-sacred* essay in 1921, he was already rowing against the tide.[325]

According to Greenslade, *'less than a decade before, the opinions of the British people had been moulded – against their prior wishes – to accept the necessity of going to war.'* But Prime-Minister, David Lloyd George, already knew the facts about the horrors of the frontline.[326] He had been advised by CP Scott himself, but the political priority was to prevent the peace movement taking hold. Lloyd George's pronouncements were accepted by Cabinet and the general British public. Britain joined the war in August 1914.

So, should we simply dispense with fact-hunting altogether?

Perhaps, there is a time and context for publishing facts – but **deviations from stating facts should be exceptional rather than the norm.** (See Chapter 1 on when to tell the truth.)

The **Leveson Inquiry** in Britain in 2011 and 2012[327] exposed not only the deliberate lies which had been published in the press but also the invasive techniques used to stalk celebrities with a view to getting potential information around which to base salacious stories. On the other hand, if there was no market for such stories, then the publishers would write differently or go out of business.

It is possible to make clear nonsense sound plausible, if it is delivered with conviction and panache. Consider this British schoolyard poem:

> It was in the month of Liverpool
> In the city of July
> The rain was snowing heavily
> And the streets were very dry.

These are all valid English language words, combined together with correct grammar and syntax. The poem has rhythm and rhyme. It flows off the tongue. Yet, it is full of logical inconsistencies, from line to line, which render it headshakingly meaningless.

How often do we hear blatant falsehoods or inconsistencies delivered with passion[328] and reported with sincere intensity on the media?[329]

It is not hard to understand that, in the emotion of a political or protest rally, people will be carried along by the words without stopping to check their logic or meaning – let alone the truth of the 'facts'.[330] Rally participants are looking to chant slogans repetitively, to believe what they are being told and to be carried along by the hysteria of the occasion.

In the current short-attention span of media presentations, the video and sound grabs often report moments just as they are recorded, apparently with minimal editorial qualification or context.[331] Then they hit the social media and go viral, frequently for comic effect.

The mantras of the campaign hustings can often be arrant nonsense, made to sound plausible by confident delivery and repetition. Rather than listeners hearing detailed researched plans, they hear what they want to hear in order to have their biases confirmed. It is also the 'availability heuristic' – if it is heard often enough, it will come to be believed.

Let us acknowledge that there are many very capable, professional journalists and editors around the world who do their due diligence in reporting facts, researching stories and presenting cogent arguments.

Their messages can, however, be lost in the morass of saturation output from a host of media outlets.

But, if you seek out and follow those quality messages <u>alone</u>, is that not another form of confirmation bias and you are entrenching your own viewpoints?

On the evidence above, it would be hard for the average readers or watchers of the media to have confidence that they are being exposed to the truth, even if it is confirming what they already think.

Much more likely, it would seem that they are being exposed to some form of manipulation of thinking which is trying to align the recipients with an argument, an ideology, a cause or a pressing expression of voting power.

Is that a moral position?

Has that type of manipulation always been there?

Perhaps the persuasive influence of schooling, preaching and social information systems has always been the main tool of those in power.

Even today, mobile phones track the owner's movements. Social media platforms create personal profiles based on click patterns on the Internet.

These profiles can then direct advertising to suit personal preferences or forward persuasive articles which may or may not be true. Each user is vulnerable to being manipulated without his/her direct knowledge.[332]

What, then, is the moral solution to that dilemma?
The reader's skill is to have sufficient critical-thinking ability – the knowledge of the persuasive fallacies – to separate reality from the fiction.

How is that skill to be imparted to the mass of the people without falling into the same manipulating traps that we have been illustrating in this chapter?

Is it morally acceptable in a civilised society to rely on the masses to sort between lies, spin and the truth?

> *Journalist: Mr Ghandi, what do you think of Western Civilisation?*
> *Ghandi: I think it would be a good idea.*
>
> **Mahatma Ghandi**[333]

Chapter 14

Is the definition of morality the prerogative of the self-righteous? Are some people naturally superior and others inferior?

My working hypothesis for this book is that every moral decision is a prisoner of its time and culture.

The previous chapters have illustrated that what is understood as the truth is not an absolute.

What is accepted as truth might depend on its use, misuse or abuse, or its era in history. The telling of lies has been justified in some cases. The manipulation of truth through fallacies has been the framing tool of propagandists for generations.

The concepts of truth, of right and wrong, of good or bad, are mental notions which imply a comparison to something.

So, for example, when we say our action is *right*, what do we really mean? *Right* compared to what?

Does it mean better than other options? Does it mean compared to a standard? What is a standard? Who creates the standard? Is it a

UDHR interpretation or the Cairo Declaration of Human Rights? Or is it some other standard from a belief system?

Our whole concept of morality depends on our personalised framework for making judgements. That would initially reflect our upbringing which would, in turn, have been influenced by thinkers in generations past and the beliefs that our particular culture held to be important. That base framework can be refined by our on-going experiences of life, our reading and our flexibility in thinking – but **our view of morality is still relative or compared to:**

- what we know – the comfort of familiarity, or
- **other options about which we might have some awareness.**

Even the wide range of traditional religions is an expression that the search for truthful meaning is an elusive target for much of mankind, generally – and can be interpreted in many, often opposing, ways.

The world of science and critical thinking has taken some understandings to new levels, particularly in medical fields, information technology and cosmology. Science deals in **the certainty of doubt** – that any current hypothesis is open for testing, ready to be challenged and to be replaced by better hypotheses, if such are available. Truth is hard to establish definitively.

Albert Einstein's great skill was to see time, gravity and space in a new way – the theory of relativity.[334] Despite Isaac Newton's theories from 1686 CE[335] having been accepted for centuries as the likely ultimate definition of gravity, Einstein couldn't fully reconcile Newtonian gravitational laws with thermodynamics and the electromagnetic field.

So he put forward alternative hypotheses for the photoelectric effect and tested them mathematically. Those discoveries led to developing the pillars of special and general relativity, while influencing the thinking around quantum theory.

Einstein actually spent much of the rest of his life trying to disprove his own theories – the certainty of doubt. Now, after many decades, Einstein's theories have been tested and accepted as the best currently available.[336] However, it is likely that they will be challenged by new theories into the future.

The offshoots of those types of research have delivered new inventions and lifted the standard of living for the wealthier countries of the world to a very comfortable level. Life for most in those countries is well beyond the level of daily survival. People in those lands have leisure time; a space to think, to learn, to write, to travel and to philosophise.

However, the misuse of a little learning has created the opportunity for theories to be used in a fallacious way.

For example, *if an idea hasn't been proved wrong, then it must be correct* is a classic logical fallacy. One does not presuppose the other.

That form of illogicality, coupled with didactic styles of social education, is the breeding ground for reversion to the simpler traditional notions of meaning and living. It is, as I implied in the working hypothesis, a process of entrenching moral thinking in the dogma of belief systems, of creating inalienable versions of untestable 'truth' which are frequently enforced by laws, regulation, punishment, re-education and suppression.

Have distortions of moral ideas become 'par for the course'?

For example, *freedom of speech* is a concept built into many social systems in order to allow alternative views to be heard and so that public leaders can be held to account.

It is a matter of doubt that the concept was ever intended to enable the powerful to abuse the less powerful. But it certainly can be used in that way.

The use of free expression is a balance which many societies have chosen to regulate, in order to prevent slander, libel, victimisation or fallacious bald lies.

Yet, the powerful in society have often tried to control media investigations and replace the findings of journalists' stories with the distractions of dubious or false propaganda. Some high-profile politicians have used reverse psychology to call the general media 'fake news' while spouting their own information which is indeed factually incorrect.[337]

But we have also noted that free speech is not a valid concept in all cultures across the planet, particularly for those who wish to suppress opposition and to control what information is given to the general population. If you hear something often enough, with no counter arguments, you will come to believe that it is correct. It is the 'availability heuristic' at work.[338]

Furthermore, the notion of rights (as opposed to responsibilities) depends on the culture of particular societies. For some, it is an aspirational ideal and for others it is more rooted in religious interpretation.

The notions of wealth and power are woven throughout all the discussions of rights.

In essence, it has been the role of those in power (chiefs, politicians, presidents, dictators) to make the rules for society. That may be through the wealth of heredity or the power of armies or the interpretation of religion or by using particular ideologies of social organisation, including lobby groups with strong vested interests.

While aspiration can be a goal to set direction, it is also important 'to practise what you preach'[339] and to live in the real world while you aspire.

As Bertrand Russell wrote in *On Education* (1926, p.127): *A truly robust morality can only be strengthened by the fullest knowledge of what really happens in the world.*[340]

In that context, let's examine the notions of people being powerful or being less powerful.

Are some people superior to others?

Do some people have 'the right answers' while others should just listen and obey?

Who decides what our morality should be?

Most of us can acknowledge talent in others.

- **Usain Bolt**[341] is a sprinter of the highest quality, having won the individual Olympic gold medals for 100 and 200 metres at three successive Olympic Games. Whether or not we are athletes, it is likely that no amount of training could help us run as fast as he can move. In that sense, he is a superior athlete.

- Likewise with physicist, **Albert Einstein** (mentioned earlier). His ability to visualise complex scientific concepts and test them with the highest level of mathematics would leave most of us shaking our heads in bewilderment. It has taken many decades for some of his projections to be confirmed. He was well ahead of his time.

- **Leonardo da Vinci**[342] was not just a talented artist but he also explored science and he conceived inventions like a flying machine and a submarine, hundreds of years before they were actually able to be built. He is generally acknowledged as an artistic and scientific talent whose influence has spanned centuries.

In these three examples, the level of extreme talent or genius is beyond the norm for our species and rare enough for the general public to recognise it as superior, without any threat.

But there is another side to seeing some people as being superior or inferior.

The American Declaration of Independence of 1776 stated:

> We hold these truths to be self-evident, that all men are created equal, that they are endowed by their Creator with certain unalienable Rights, that among these are Life, Liberty and the pursuit of Happiness.[343]

This was an aspirational document for a new country.

It is notable that 'all men' did not acknowledge the equality of women nor that many of the signatories on the document were slave owners at the time of signing … or that the subsequent legal system of the United States of America not only prevented the equality of African-Americans but it also prevented marriage between whites and non-whites, through the anti-miscegenation laws until 1967.[344]

Colonial powers throughout history have used military power to conquer others, to plunder resources and to enslave populations. It was seen to be the correct order of things in Roman times, in Viking times also and right up to the empires of Spain, France and Britain. That might have been alright if you were the slave owner. However, the slaves probably had a different view.

Skin colour and lifestyle were taken to identify people who were seen as being inferior to the superiority of the conquering nations. That attitude was reinforced, not just in the rules of society, but also in the manipulation of ideas.

The Christian missionaries of the 18th and 19th centuries believed that **they were bringing religion and civilisation to lesser people** – helping the savage or primitive man.[345] Whatever the zeal and personal commitment of the individual missionaries, the larger agenda was about increasing commerce and wealth for the colonisers. That also required training that subjugated people – assimilating them to the culture of the invaders – at least to the extent that they could be useful.

A Philosophical Morality Challenge

In terms of morality, seen through 21st century eyes, the colonising model was self-righteous and used all the tools of military subjugation and re-education to establish that the rulers were superior and that the ruled were born to be inferior.

That process was reinforced by the illusion of wealth for the superior ones, and generous scraps for the 'grateful' inferior ones.

Were the colonists superior?

Probably not, as individuals. At the time, their culture had superior weapons along with the concepts of industry and expanding commerce.

And, as discussed in Chapter 11, there is an historical catalogue of the mass of 'inferiors' overthrowing the 'superiors'. That happened because those masses could no longer accept power and wealth to be the privilege of a very few (cf. French revolution 1789–99 CE).

Even within colonising countries such as 19th century industrial Britain, **the superior wealth was an illusion for the majority**. Smoky, squalid back-to-back terraces of the British industrial revolution were testimony to lives of cramped housing and long days of labour for the working class.[346] When the fraud of superiority was finally revealed in the colonies, the people accepted that they could and should revolt in an attempt to remove their oppressors (cf. Indian mutiny 1857 CE). But not all revolutions ended well for the oppressed.

This control of the masses by persuasion, illusion and political manipulation is happening to this day.

- In some cases, it is the power of military intimidation and physical punishment (including execution and genocide)

that constrains the ability of the people to remove the rulers and to share the prosperity of the land.
- It could be the manipulation of political processes to entrench the status quo (see Chapter 16).
- In other cases, the colonisation is actually being carried out by global companies who can use their wealth to influence legal systems to their advantage.

What about the superiority of force?
Gangsters, famously, have used force to break the rules of society.

Legends, perhaps apocryphal stories, have grown up about many such outlaws, bushrangers and highwaymen. For example, Robin Hood became renowned for stealing from the rich and giving to the poor. But, in most actual cases, gangsters are after power … and a sense of belonging to an untouchable gang.

It could be the **Ku Klux Klan** (KKK) of the United States of America[347] who abused and murdered African Americans through the 19th and 20th centuries, justified as some self-righteous sense of superiority of white people and as a protest against the mainstream country's direction. At some level, the KKK members were using the Bible along with fantasies in book[348] and film form[349], to justify their superiority.

It could be the **Daech/ISIS** group of the 21st century in Iraq and Syria,[350] invading large areas and establishing a particularly brutal rule. Ostensibly, they were using a fundamentalist interpretation of Islam to justify their colonisation of the land and its peoples. They were also involved in the enslavement and extermination of resistors or non-acceptors.[351]

It could be the **'White Australia' policy** of the 20th century[352] which was intended to create a utopian society for white people only … and to remove any other races.

A Philosophical Morality Challenge

The idea was that the white people were superior and that they belonged together. The notion was fostered by Britain's migration policy and its need to get access to the primary resources of a large continent. The 'White Australia' policy was justified because the politicians who made the laws were **looking after what they believed was in their self-interest**.

The policy was backed up by legislation and force – by refusing visas to non Anglo-Saxons and by forcibly removing the Aboriginal people to mission reserves where they were out of sight and educated only to Grade 4 level.[353] Some children were part of an assimilation process, occasionally placed either with non-Aboriginal families or brought up in strictly run dormitories on the missions.

By the start of World War II, Australia was made up of 99 per cent white people,[354] of British or Northern European origin, although the presence of others (Aboriginals, Torres Strait Islanders, Chinese, Japanese, Kanakas[355]) was probably only a scarcely regarded estimate on the censuses, if measured at all.

However, after the invasion scares in World War II, Australia embarked on a massive immigration program from all parts of Europe. In 1947, Australian Minister for Immigration, Arthur Calwell, said to critics of mass immigration from non-British Europe: *'We have 25 years at most to populate this country before the yellow races are down on us'*[356] – such was the alienation of the time, particularly towards Asian countries. That changed after the Vietnam War and the disbanding of the 'White Australia' policy between 1965 to 1973.

While the Australia of the 21st century is a very successful, multi-ethnic society with many people tracing their ancestries back to non Anglo-Saxon countries, the legacies of the 'White Australia' government policy continue to this day in attitudes of superiority which are close to the surface of public debate. There are isolationist attitudes towards non Anglo-Saxon migrants and refugees, which is reflected in some polling support for any politicians who espouse those protectionist views.

Overall, the disadvantage to the descendants of the First Australians – the Aboriginal people – continues. They still suffer from earlier deaths, higher incarceration levels and greater social disadvantage.[357]

And yet, the catalogue of highly successful individual Aboriginal people in Australia includes doctors, lawyers, university professors, teachers, school principals, business owners, writers, pilots, soldiers, senior police officers, singers, magistrates, television producers, sports people and a state governor, as well as federal and state politicians.

As these examples attest ...

> ***The success is most likely not to do with any individual superiority of race or culture. It is more to do with opportunity, particularly with ready access to quality education and to remove the covert barriers to social independence rather than dependence.***

Is this notion of superior culture in any way genetic?
The **eugenics** movement of the 19th and 20th centuries went to great lengths to try to prove that some people were genetically superior to others.[358] Sir Francis Galton (1822–1911) tried to build on the ideas of his half-cousin, Charles Darwin in his *Origin of Species*.[359]

Darwin wrote about natural selection. Galton added a new twist and argued that the natural selection process was being thwarted by civilisation. He reasoned that the underprivileged and the weak were being protected by the morality of the times and that was at odds with natural selection ... and, indeed, with the past accepted moral practice of the Greek and Roman times.[360] Galton argued that genius and talent were hereditary traits and artificial selection could produce a highly gifted race by judicious marriages over several generations.

These 19th century academic views were seized upon during the reign of Nazi Germany, with a range of experiments being tried on concentration camp inmates and with breeding programs being instituted in order to produce a pure Aryan race.

After the Nuremberg war crime trials, eugenics became almost universally reviled. The UN Universal Declaration of Human Rights has replaced the eugenics arguments, although the world of genetic engineering continues with minimal controversy in animal breeding, genetically-modified plant development and IVF.

Let us finally deal with attitudes towards people with a disability. Without doubt, there are many with disabilities in all societies who would not survive without considerable carer and community support. It is the government policy in most developed countries to provide assistance to those in need.

There are also many who have disabilities and who do lead very successful lives, in spite of their disadvantage. You need only look at the successful athletes at Paralympic Games, who demonstrate impressive skills. Likewise, the Invictus Games give opportunities to military personnel who have been injured in conflict zones.

But more ... **what is a disability?**

How do we measure it?

Are the savants, the mathematical and artistic geniuses of this world, disabled?[361] The general public can only marvel at their skills.

The loss of one sense or capability can often mean the development of other senses. What about colour blindness? The ability to not to be confused by green colour can enable a soldier to see through normal camouflage.

There have certainly been times in human history when any disability would have a person viewed as inferior. But there are so many examples in the modern world of successful people who have lived with disability as loving children and parents. They went on to drive cars, to fly planes, to be television personalities or to just bring the joy of their personalities to family members and friends.

It is often how disability is measured and understood.
I observed a girl in a wheelchair at a sports carnival in country Queensland. She could not participate in the normal events because she was the only one in a wheelchair. But the organisers of the carnival borrowed five wheelchairs from the local hospital and staged a wheelchair race for the girl against five able-bodied athletes of her age, over a grass track.

The wheelchair girl won the 100 metre race by many metres.

No explanation was needed for the cheering watchers and an important lesson in understanding was learned, without a word needing to be spoken.

So, what does this mean for morality?
If disabled people had been born in the ancient Greek eras, the morality of that time would not have let them survive.[362] The morality of the 21st century, in most developed countries, provides regulations which protect children once they are born, no matter what their talents or challenges.

To a large extent, the communication and education techniques of this age can alert the majority of the world's population to the discriminatory policies of past ages ... and make them aware of international moral expectations. There are anti-discrimination laws in most countries and the UN Declaration of Human Rights emphasises that principle to protect the vulnerable and to maximise opportunity for everyone.

Views on morality do change with time.

A Philosophical Morality Challenge

Forty years ago there were many ethical protests to IVF (joining an egg and sperm outside the body before transferring the embryo to the woman's uterus to increase the chance that pregnancy will occur), especially when the first test tube baby was born in 1978. The protestors were arguing that: Man was playing God. It would be a slippery slope. Where would it all end? Should health services pay for it? How would the recipients be prioritised?

The ethical challenges and discussions are still here but, today, without the passionate protests. IVF is now a routine procedure with millions of children being born worldwide through this process, without public concern.[363] The context has moved on. The morality has been accepted by the majority.

Morality is a shifting feast. It has meant different things over time and context.

With respect to disability, most attitude changes come from familiarity with individuals, with appreciating their personal qualities, with understanding people's personalities and not fearing their difference ... it is about education and humanity in their broadest senses.

Frans de Waal, the Dutch primate scholar, suggests that humans are:

'both more systematically brutal than chimps and more empathic than bonobos [monkeys]. We are by far the most bipolar ape. Our societies are never completely peaceful, never completely competitive, never ruled by sheer selfishness, and never perfectly moral.'[364]

That is an interesting observation on humans and the indefinite nature of our sense of morality.

Based on the evidence in this chapter, it is unlikely that there is mass genetic superiority of peoples or that the self-righteous have any grounds for a superior stance on morality.

THE MOST AVOIDED QUESTIONS

A little learning is a dang'rous thing
Alexander Pope

Chapter 15

Is survival of the species more important than human rights?

Societies that have traditionally operated near the survival zone tend to develop cultural priorities to ensure that the tribe survives.

- For example, in traditional **Inuit** society in the Arctic regions, the food supply was seasonal and not reliable. It depended on catching seal, whale or fish. The culture had established protocols as to how the catch was to be distributed among the community … and that was generally geared towards keeping the hunters fit and strong … and the women rearing healthy children. In hard times in Inuit society, it was not unknown for aged people to be allowed to pass away honourably – suicide – so that there would be enough food for the others.[365]

- Similar examples can be found in the animal world. The **penguin rookeries** off the coast of Peru depend on the Humboldt Current to bring fish to feed the colony. The current is not always dependable and commercial fishing has reduced the fish stocks. In the years when the fish are not plentiful, the adult penguins abandon many of their chicks and allow them to die, so ensuring that there will be enough fish for the colony to survive into the next season.[366]

- In **Spartan society**, in ancient Greece, they managed the births of children by elders making decisions about the viability of the child to be productive. In the culture and context of their time, they needed warriors to defend their militaristic lifestyle and healthy women to produce more children. Babies who didn't fit that mould would be left on the hillside to die.[367]

These three examples highlight the priorities in different types of social groupings which for varying reasons are, or were, living near the survival level. **The decisions were made on the basis of the tribe or group surviving.**

That is a very different perspective on human rights from that espoused by Universal Declaration of Human Rights or the UN Declaration on the Rights of the Child[368] or the debates in courts, parliaments or congresses on the rights of the elderly to choose how they might end their lives.[369]

In 1974, ecologist **Garrett Hardin**[370] introduced the lifeboat scenario[371] as a metaphor for an ethical dilemma.

In Hardin's metaphor, he describes a lifeboat containing fifty people and with space for only ten more. The boat is in an ocean surrounded by one hundred swimmers.

On what basis should swimmers be taken on board the lifeboat?

Hardin then compared his lifeboat metaphor with his Spaceship Earth model of planetary resource distribution where the rich nations were the lifeboats and the swimmers were the poor nations.

The moral questions (what **you** should do in the situation) are enormous, such as:

- What criteria would you use to accept a swimmer on board?
- Would it be the first to reach the boat?
- Or perhaps it could be someone who could help the whole boat survive?

- Or might it be the person most in need?
- Would you deny help to an obviously dying person so that others would have a better chance to survive?
- Do you jettison a dying person to make room for someone else?
- Would you engage in cannibalism to survive?

Variations of this scenario are used in many business training sessions on how decisions could and should be made. They help the participants tease out their own moral positions for their businesses and for the wider ethical priorities about living in society.

The ethical questions (the general moral principles that **society** should endorse as appropriate behaviour, often by regulations or laws) might be around social attitudes to the acceptance of the survival decisions that the lifeboat people might make in extreme circumstances, **in contrast to unregulated self-interest**.

Hardin's metaphor highlights the challenges for decision making in dire situations. In his mind, it relates to environmental ethics, resource depletion and population expansion. He questioned the morality of the accepted humanitarian policies such as foreign aid, immigration and food banks. He was choosing the 'bigger picture' survival of the species and natural selection, over the compassionate individualistic caring for people in difficulties.

In the context of Spaceship Earth, is it alright for capitalist interests to plunder the Earth's resources for personal gain?

Is it alright for parliaments of people to debate, deliberate and obfuscate while a potential ecological tragedy unfolds?

There is a host of environmental writers, particularly from the 1960s, who flagged the real and potential outcomes of unrestricted economic policies, particularly when they involved impacts on natural ecosystems. They were such writers as Rachel Carson who wrote *Silent Spring* (1966),[372] Garrett Hardin who wrote *The Tragedy of the Commons* (1968),[373] Lynn White's *The Historical Roots of our*

Ecological Crisis (1967)[374] and the revival of Aldo Leopold's *A Sand County Almanac* (1947).[375]

Yet, world governments have had great difficulty agreeing on a united approach to global environmental concerns, especially when their competitive streaks see an economic disadvantage for their powerful business backers. Letting go of some national self-interest is a hard concept for many politicians to handle.

The 2015 Paris UN conference on climate change was a rare example of some success, after many failures and compromises.[376] The proof of success will be how well countries abide by their pledged commitments into the future, as economic pressures start to bite.

Using Hardin's Spaceship Earth metaphor, Earth would need a Spaceship Captain (that is a global leader with the capacity to make decisions for us all). **So, would it be alright for a Spaceship Captain – which Earth lacks – to take control and make decisions based on survival?**

As a world, we have not had to face such an all-encompassing prospect as world survival (not based on the threat of nuclear war) until relatively recently. **It is a new moral context.**

At present, a range of G7 to G20 heads of government groups try to reach consensus around world directions but world survival as such is a rare matter of discussion on their agendas.[377]

If we had a Spaceship Captain, there would **need to be many checks and balances on the power** and the length of tenure.

In the words of 19th century English historian and writer, Lord Acton,[378] '*Power tends to corrupt and absolute power corrupts absolutely. Great men are almost always bad men, even when they exercise influence and not authority: still more when you superadd the tendency or the certainty of corruption by authority*'.[379]

As Lord Acton suggested, it is hard to find any examples in history of successful, long-term, one-person leadership. Nearly always it degenerates into brutal dictatorship. There are many historical examples of narcissistic, out-of-control despots who fell prey to the lure of absolute power, while ignoring the need for mass survival (e.g. Stalin, Hitler, Mussolini … and many more modern dictatorial versions in Africa, the Middle East, South America and Asia[380]).

What is the moral solution to this dilemma of unrestricted rights and inadequate global leadership around responsibility?

At what point, does the survival of the species take precedence over the rights of individuals or corporations or religions or nations?

Clearly, that is a problem fraught with lots of vested interests and, to a considerable extent, many of those same vested interests control the democratic decision making processes.

So, is it possible for sensible, researched arguments to hold sway with the current decision makers?

The short answer on the evidence is, 'Yes'. But the leadership required is generally well above the norm.

African philosophers speak of Ubuntu.[381]

Ubuntu is an African ethic of care (not a religion) which emphasises human interdependence. It comes out of the rural environments where no-one is anonymous. It is a philosophy that recognises that we belong together and that we all have rights and responsibilities. It encompasses the notion of a social conscience.[382]

Ubuntu has a communitarian understanding of moral justice, to which **Nelson Mandela** referred in many speeches,[383] to encourage people to make justice their prime moral concern.

It is a compassionate system which replaces violence, bigotry and aggression with empathy, love, unity and humility – skills which must actually be taught and learned or they are just slogans.

The Truth and Reconciliation Commission (TRC) in South Africa,[384] which began in 1994, is an example of Ubuntu justice.

It amazed many people in the world at the time by its firm yet gentle approach – rather than the potential blood bath if Nelson Mandela had decried the great injustices of the past.

Ubuntu justice is moral, compassionate and restorative.

The 'truth telling' at the TRC about past human atrocities and the listening to testimonies from those who sought amnesty or reparation together formed a way to realise justice. It forced people to take responsibility and to understand the impact of their actions. That is a very different style and philosophy to many of the justice systems that operate in other parts of the world.

To some extent, it resolved part of a potential powder keg following the 'apartheid' era.[385] It didn't encourage revenge and retribution but rather offered compassion, forgiveness and healing in a culture of human dignity. **And it took Nelson Mandela's leadership approach, as a South African role model and president, to achieve it.**

It would be easy to dismiss this as airy-fairy idealism which can't succeed in the face of a warlike enemy or terrorism.

But, stop and consider.

This is a contrasting approach to that taken by Allied countries in the *crimes against humanity* trials after World War II. Indeed, even the approaches to the treatment of Nazis and those of the Japanese Empire varied markedly, over time.

For those indicted as part of Nazi Germany, the Nuremberg War Crime Trials[386] gave a forum for information about the atrocities of the regime to be shared and for the accused to have their say. Then sentences were announced and carried out. Other German trials were conducted in the years after … and they continue to this day, following up on any who might be indicted for crimes committed tens of decades before.[387]

For those indicted as part of the Japanese Empire in World War II, there were similar trials, sentences and executions in the immediate aftermath of the war.

But, on 4 September 1952, US President Harry S. Truman signed an executive order, # 10393, which established a Clemency and Parole Board for convicted Japanese war criminals.[388] Many were released on parole in 1954 under President Dwight D. Eisenhower's supplementary orders to # 10393 and by the end of 1958 all Japanese war criminals had been released, with clemency or an amnesty announced by the Allies.[389] There have been no more trials nor sentences for Japanese war criminals since.

Reputedly, that amnesty action was started on the advice of US General Douglas MacArthur to President Truman, in 1950.

MacArthur had been in charge of post-war Japanese reconstruction and was, by 1950, leading the UN military campaign in the Korean War. Allegedly, he wanted the Japanese war consigned to the past and to consolidate Japan as a peaceful base; a bulwark against the communist forces during, and after, the Korean conflict.[390]

If this is true, here was an example of a 'Spaceship Earth Captain' being able to influence a president of the United States who, it is known, personally railed at allowing MacArthur to behave like a supreme commander. Indeed, Truman dismissed him as the military commander in Korea on 11 April 1951.

But, without MacArthur's impetus, it would be hard to see how the amnesty outcome would have progressed in the aftermath of the Pacific and Asian war, such was the pain and hostility felt towards the Japanese by returned troops and the families of those who had lost relatives and friends in action during World War II.

There certainly was no similar amnesty in Germany where the United States had a similar post-war influence. But, with assertive leadership, a major change can happen.

So, in terms of getting decisions made for the survival of the planet, we have seen three different approaches to resolving the aftermath of horrendous crimes – the TRC in South Africa, plus the German and Japanese war crimes trials.

Consequently, **when dealing with whether or not the survival of the species might take precedence over vested interests, it is a problem that is not necessarily in the too-hard basket.** The challenge is to get the decision making processes to appreciate the nature and scale of the problem.

In the words attributed to Nelson Mandela …

> ***'It always seems impossible until it is done.'***[391]

We will return to this concept in Chapter 17. It is a matter of getting an understanding of priorities.

As Alexander Solzhenitzen wrote in *One day in the Life of Ivan Denisovich*, 'How can you expect a man who's warm to understand a man who's cold?'[392]

The survival of the species is a similar problem.

> ***Decision makers who have no experience of life on the edge – and who enjoy the fruits of capitalist success – can have minimal understanding of 'the man who's cold'.***

Or that the freight train of ecosystem collapse might be coming towards them, silently, but with speed. Life is too easy and profitable to worry about the most avoided questions.

The grass must bend when the wind blows across it.
Confucius

Chapter 16

Are we all brainwashed and the notion of free will is a myth?

In the 1970s, Benjamin Libet of the University of California conducted famous experiments which suggested that neural responses could be detected before the mental instruction was given to move a wrist or a finger.[393] The participants had a free choice to make the move whenever they wanted. That led some researchers to theorise that:

> **Unconscious processes in the brain can initiate volitional responses.**

In 1999, Harvard University psychologists, Dan Wegner and Thalia Wheatley,[394] suggested that humans trick themselves into thinking that they have free will to make decisions. They stated that:

'The experience of intentionally willing an action is often no more than a post hoc causal inference that our thoughts caused the behaviour.'[395]

Yale University academics, Adam Bear and Paul Bloom have research results which suggest that the brain rewrites history when it makes choices, changing our memories so that we believe that we wanted to do something before it actually happened. The researchers, however, added careful caveats that the illusion of choice might only apply to choices made quickly.[396]

Professor Alex Rosenberg,[397] in *The Atheist's Guide to Reality*, extrapolates those ideas to declare that the brain is primarily a sequence of chemical reactions to stimuli over which we have minimal control. He uses his argument to support his views on scientism[398] and the theory of natural selection.

He also delves into the morality debate with the suggestion that *'the core morality that mother nature imposed on us, together with the denial of free will, is bound to make the consistent thinker sympathetic to a left-wing, egalitarian agenda about the treatment of criminals and of billionaires.'*[399] Perhaps neither group had a choice to become one or the other. It was all bound to happen – unavoidable.

That is one side of the argument – that the evolutionary path has programmed many thinking sequences into our brains and that we dupe ourselves to believe that it is our conscious mind at work.

Another part of a similar argument against free will is that society trains the mass of people to be passive and accepting of whatever social order they are living in.

In Chapter 10, we discussed the mind-controlling practices of cults. In Chapters 8 and 9, we mentioned the socialisation process to support the current economic theories and the accrual of wealth. We have philosopher and writer, Iris Murdoch (1919–1999), suggesting that the moral decisions that you might make will be determined by your upbringing to this point.

Many cultures regard obedience as a virtue. The notion is inculcated through community expectation, the schooling systems, the corrective services and the religious organisations. Karl Marx is often quoted as saying that religion was 'the opiate of the masses' (a frequent translation from his words) because of its requirement to submit to the will of God. The term Islam, also, can mean 'surrender' to the will of Allah.[400]

Karl Marx's actual written quote was *'Religion is the sigh of the oppressed creature, the heart of a heartless world, and the soul of soulless conditions. It is the opium of the people.'* [401] His concern was, as he saw it, that religion was a human construct and that the interpretations of deific will were a means of pacifying people into accepting their lot in life. Marx was also concerned about other economic and political constructs that he saw oppressing people.

Religion is but one of the social influences that drive compliance. Social influence is the effect that the words, actions, or the mere presence of other people (real or imagined) can have on our thoughts, feelings, attitudes, or behaviour.

Persuasion and the gaining of compliance are significant types of socialisation because the effect is to gain the submission of others.

The Stanford Prison experiment[402] in 2011 asked for volunteers to be locked up in Stanford County Jail in California for a number of days; some as inmates, some as guards.

The jail was in fact an illusion – set up in a laboratory near the actual prison, made up with bars and cell numbers to resemble the real jail. The participants were brought blindfolded into the facility.

In the experiment, the 'inmates' were subjected to normal prison routines such as liberty deprivation, loss of identity, being woken for head counts and being sprayed for lice.

At the end of the experiment, 'inmates' reported feelings of humiliation, loss of dignity and being just a number. 'Guards' became immersed in the power of their roles, despite any earlier moral or social values. Both parties quickly complied with the assumed authority that their different roles implied.

The experiment showed the power of perception in inducing compliance to assumed social positions. **It is about how reality is framed.** In the view of the researchers, free will did not appear to be a chosen option in this experiment. The participants adapted quickly to the expectations of their roles. They didn't rebel – and yet it was all an illusion.

Or … a contrasting view might argue that the experiment actually **is** free will being exercised by each in complying to a social expectation – they were choosing to belong? It is a moot point.

Transfer that type of socialisation into the world in which we live.

How much freedom and independence of thought do we actually have?

One interpretation of socialisation is that it can be seen as humans using their free will to fit into a social group, as they choose.

Our whole concept of morality is based on the human's ability to pick between right and wrong. Yet, our thinking might be subject to significant manipulation by speech or circumstance, by social influences.[403]

How does the range of varying viewpoints on morality (illustrated in earlier chapters) sit with the notion that our thinking might be unconsciously determined?

Free will is the foundation of our thinking about philosophy. *Have we just been kidding ourselves?*

Or … could we take the view that deterministic arguments that deny free will are just convenient excuses to use isolated examples of apparently spontaneous neural reactions to extrapolate that all our thinking is merely a chemical response to stimuli? Extrapolating the part to assume the same for the whole on such a sample would be a fallacy of composition. *As critical thinkers, we would challenge that logic.*

Isn't most thinking coerced in some way?

Martin Seligman,[404] a research psychologist of Pennsylvania University, has written extensively about *learned helplessness*, which is a response to repeated adverse stimuli from which the person cannot escape (e.g. child abuse by neglect). That can express itself as depression, a victim mentality or helpless dependency. In essence, it is a mental health condition inflicted by social influences – caused by coercion.

But surely not all actions in life are coerced, unconsciously or socially predetermined?

Without coercion, can we think freely?

Our legal approach to culpability holds that perpetrators have had the ability to make choices ... and, therefore, society has the right to choose to punish or to acquit on the same basis.

It has been an assumed truth for generations that perpetrators have exercised freedom of thought, unless mental illness (e.g. Seligman's example above) can be established and accepted by the courts.

> ***The legal principle of mens rea[405] (a guilty mind) requires prosecutors to prove that a culpable action was both conscious and voluntary.***

That presupposes *'that we have free will – that we are not caused to do what we do by matters outside our control, but rather in any situation we have real choices between alternative courses of action which are truly open to us, in the sense that, given the situation and even given our own natures and characters, it is truly possible for us to take any one of these alternatives'.*[406]

Most of the scientific research in this 'free will' area, since Libet, has focused on automatic neurological responses to specific stimuli.[407]

- There have been a lot of assumptions which flow from these simple tests which are yet to be established beyond reasonable doubt.
- In addition, from a scientific method approach, the experiments have been conducted to measure responses to single

types of stimuli. We have not yet developed measures for the complexities of free thinking.

Dr Mahir S Ozdemir, a biomedical engineer from Belgium, **challenges the fundamental cause and effect assumption of these simple neural tests.** That is the assumption that if free will is involved then the physical reaction should happen exactly when the mental stimulus is given – not before or long after.[408]

Ozdemir contends that thinking processes are in a continuum and that the much-quoted experiments merely show that thinking was occurring before the stimulus. Indeed, Ozdemir considers that the observation is only showing that thinking is a complex series of processes. He rejects the assumption that the tests automatically suggest that there was an unconscious cause and effect reaction or that the person was duped about the freedom of choice.

Furthermore, he argues that all the deterministic experiments so far have had the participants being aware of the likely expectations – which raises questions to him about validity. He says that, despite only simple mechanical timing reactions being observed, there have been large leaps in the assumptions of what those tests might actually mean.

In his view, the researchers present no evidence to support their assumption that the particular brain activity applicable to their experiment happens without conscious decisions being made. It is an over-simplified extrapolation that any brain activity happening before an action must be the cause of an anticipated effect.

Finally, Ozdemir contends that complex thinking is not a simple binary decision and he further argues that the 'no-free-will' case has not been made. **In his view, there is a large gap in the logical reasoning** – the premises for the conclusion are not valid or even strong – to the extent that the claims are exaggerated and must be rebutted.

A Philosophical Morality Challenge

In 1984, philosopher and author, Professor Daniel Dennett, wrote in *Elbow Room*[409] about **the complexity of the neural processes**. He argued that free will and science can be compatible; that there can be gradations of consciousness in that there are some subconscious reactions to certain stimuli. But he considered that human choice, or free will, exists in a much more general sense; that we are not as strictly genetically programmed as simple creatures, such as a wasp or a lobster or a starfish.[410] Humans **can respond**, as distinct from just react. That is the difference between viewing free will through the lens of evolutionary biology instead of physics. As part of evolution, humans can anticipate, can consider responses. They **can be responsible for**, and control, actions that they take.[411]

In later years, Dennett has spoken about competence and comprehension – one leading to another (not necessarily in that order) – in such activities as, for example, a person's ability to evaluate and sign legal contracts. He argues that there is free will and choice at work there across a range of options.

In *Consciousness Explained* in 1992,[412] Dennett wrote, *'all varieties of perception – indeed all varieties of thought or mental activity – are accomplished in the brain by parallel, multi-track processes of interpretation and elaboration of sensory inputs. Information entering the nervous system is under continuous editorial revision'.* (p.111)[413]

This constant editing and re-editing process appears akin to some of the points about neural complexity, raised above by Mahir Ozdemir.

In recent years, Dennett has engaged in regular academic debates[414] with Dr Sam Harris,[415] a renowned writer and critic of religions, who appears to attribute unconscious and conscious responses to background causes, rather than a libertarian free will.[416] Yet, Harris concedes that even without free will (by his definition), consciousness still has an important role to play in the choices we make.

These are subtle distinctions about the meaning of terminology – not easy for any layman to follow and even harder to test.

In Harris's view, his realisation about the human mind does not necessarily undermine moral responsibility or diminish the importance of social and political freedom, but it could change the way we think about some of the most important questions in life.[417] Perhaps, this is more like Alex Rosenberg's argument (mentioned earlier in this chapter).

The jury is out! The beauty of science and philosophy is that there is always doubt and theories will continue to be suggested, questioned and tested. Debate and academic challenge is a healthy process in advancing our understanding and accepted knowledge.

From a morality perspective, is our perception of right and wrong beyond our conscious control? Is it being conditioned by the particular expectations of the society in which we live?

In the pragmatic real world, socially and legally, our moral decisions are considered to be matters of free choice to anticipate, to engage or to avoid. Sane people can be, and are, held accountable for those decisions that they make.

Blind belief in authority is the greatest enemy of truth

Albert Einstein

Chapter 17

Democracy is a term used to describe a country run by the people, of the people and for the people.[418]
Is that what it really is?

In earlier chapters, we have discussed how the democratic processes work through elections, representatives and debating chambers – on the principle that the majority vote will rule.

In this chapter, let us concentrate on how well the system works.

> *In principle, everyone of voting age in a democracy should have one vote ... and all votes should have equal value to elect representatives or to record opinion in referendums.*

Then, in the parliament or the congress or the assembly, each representative can present the views of the electors and the majority opinion will carry the day.

The notion of democracy dates back to Greece in the 5th and 6th centuries BCE.[419] There were many critics of the ancient model in terms of who could qualify to vote or the quality of the people chosen to represent. But, by the 20th century, the principles of representative democracy had been embraced across much of the world as the preferred model for governance.

The United States of America has a constitutional republic.[420] The founding fathers framed the constitution to have a separation of the powers of government between the legislative (the House of Representative and the Senate), executive (the President and the White House) and judicial functions (the independent courts). They also built in a range of checks and balances so that no one function could reign supreme.

The United Kingdom has a representative parliamentary democracy under a constitutional monarchy.[421] The prime minister and government carry out executive functions on behalf and by the consent of the monarch. The legislative function is conducted in the directly-elected House of Commons, with review in the House of Lords.

The composition of the latter house was originally a chamber of hereditary landed gentry, life peers and Lords Spiritual (religious appointees) but that configuration has progressively changed since 1999.

Now, in a chamber of potentially 760 people, there are Lords Temporal, who have no hereditary or aristocratic background and are appointed by the government of the day for their lifetime only. They sit with ninety-two hereditary peers, elected from amongst the previous holders of seats. There are also the Lords Spiritual who represent the different areas of the Church of England.

Most democracies across the world largely follow these systems, with minor variations in terminology and practice. It would seem to be a reasonably fair representative process.

Yet, **electoral boundaries** don't include the same number of people – so that sparsely populated areas are not swamped by the views of the urban areas.

In principle, that could also be seen as equity at work.

However, many of the states in the USA to this day use the 'gerrymandering' system. 'Gerrymander' [422] is an American term for an electoral process which actually allows the state legislators (the politicians) to decide district boundaries and enable them to distort the effect of voting patterns to favour the re-election of particular political parties.[423]

That means that all votes are far from equal.

Governments are formed by political parties or coalitions of parties which gain most votes in the lower house. However, some countries like Denmark, the Netherlands and Canada have frequently had minority governments, not even coalitions of parties, which have worked quite effectively – largely because of the accepted norms of behaviour and the ability to negotiate deals.[424]

The upper house, or **house of review, might be based on proportional representation** (as in the Australian Senate).

In the United States, there is an Electoral College, which is the process to elect the president and vice president. The Electoral College consists of 538 electors, allocated one for each member of the House of Representatives and two for each senator. Consequently, the winner of the popular presidential vote can lose the ballot in the electoral college and fail to be elected to the top office (as in 2016 and 2000).

The political parties generally have policies which they take to an election, often based on the ideology of their party. The laws, that are generated, go through both Houses for approval.

While a majority usually means more than 50 per cent at elections or voting divisions, at referendums it could be as high as 70 per cent in a vote for constitutional change, with other conditions also applying because that type of vote will alter the fundamental nature of the organising principles of government.

Most countries are scrupulous about preventing fraud or intimidation at election time so that the elected representatives will be an accurate reflection of the people's voting wishes.

The political parties are influenced by lobby groups, who try to persuade both individual members and whole parties by their arguments ... and often by their financial support. Most democratic governments have disclosure laws which show, to the public, who has donated money.

From time to time, corruption is alleged or proved which indicates that legislative decisions have the potential to be bought. The disclosure laws are not always transparent enough.

Since elections are usually expensive exercises, the threat that lobby groups might withhold financial support or, alternatively, support another party can have a powerful impact on politicians who wish to retain their seats at the next election.

Furthermore, **most parties force their members to stick to a party line of voting.** Indeed, party whips[425] ensure that no member strays. So the representative function of a member is not necessarily what the majority of electors might have chosen.

> ***So, the democratic process is not flawless but it is generally, in principle, 'a country run by the people, of the people and for the people'.***

However, if we consider the issues from Chapter 15 and that many of the debates in parliaments, assemblies and congresses are susceptible to just being talk-fests which achieve relatively little – where the politicians are not understanding the scale or gravity of what the issues mean to the ordinary voters[426] – then there is a whole range of delaying tactics which can hold up potential legislation, such as the **filibuster.**[427]

Current political processes have been **characterised by aggressive oppositional tactics** so that cross-party support is stymied. Such processes have annoyed and disenchanted the voting public who see a wealth disparity increasing and that the politicians have been part of maintaining that disadvantage for the many.

Recent elections in the USA and Australia, along with the referendum on whether the UK should leave the European Union, have been characterised by votes for change or for minor parties in upper houses, and for no more of the old policies that are not working for so many.

> *If the need for the planet is to get agreement on economic and environmental morality, it is not likely to happen easily with the current processes.*

Democracy, in principle, deals in majorities or consensus (where most can accept a bill after having had their say, even if they are not in full agreement). Or it may deal in groupthink; where most are intimidated so that they will not oppose. They go along with the view without having aired their own views. This is more a characteristic of military dictatorships, which are sometimes disguised as democracies.

How then can decision makers be persuaded by argument, rather than the donations of lobby groups?

> *Individual politicians are often hard working, unappreciated representatives of their electors.*

But, as a group and as part of political process, the **sense of entitlement** coupled to **alienation** from the grass roots and the **priority to retain their seats** at the next election, makes them vulnerable to powerful non-elected influences.

As mentioned in earlier chapters, the law-making politicians are frequently the products of the same schools of thought which value the accumulation of personal wealth above other priorities.

Change is likely to come through a series of avenues – one series is very unpleasant and another more palatable.

The unpleasant avenues include:
- **revolution** (as in the French, Russian and Chinese revolutions) where the public can no longer tolerate not being heard or not being treated fairly.
- It can also include a **voter swing** to replace a government peacefully. However, in the current climate of party policies gravitating to the middle ground, any new option is not necessarily going to be much different from that which is being replaced.

Irrespective of whether it is a violent or peaceful revolution, the countries will be in various degrees of unpleasant turmoil and protest, as the change occurs.

The more pleasant approach is to change what is currently considered to be acceptable as political debate.
- Much of the current argumentative antagonism and political theatre is promoted by media channels as 'great television'. **Yet, real debates have rules which are intended to allow a respectful listening to logical arguments.** That is not what is happening at present. 'Political speak' [428] has become a series of meaningless 'doublespeak' [429] and clichés, with politicians being prisoners of the media cycle.
- The news grabs set out to highlight any confrontational sensation or 'rule in/rule out' **gotcha situations** because the media channels believe that will draw viewers, thereby generating ratings and advertising revenue. The theatre of such events encourages political actors to speak and perform in over-dramatised fashions, in the hope that their antics will be noticed.
- Likewise, the political commentariat generally live in **a bubble of self-sustaining circular discussion.** To some in the public, it might seem like the mob encouraging a

schoolyard fight. The only problem is that there is no school principal coming along to nip it in the bud. Indeed, the arbiter in this unseemly contest is actually the public – the ones who can vote and influence elections – or who choose not to read or listen to the commentariat.

The popular rise of **social media** is no doubt the result of many influences but, in part, it is likely to be because people can actually have a say without much censorship, can share opinions and read other points of view. While social media is derided by some (perhaps with a degree of merit), it is – in its own way – a revolution.

The Arab Spring uprisings in Africa and the Middle East over recent decades spread their communication on social media, where there was no censorship control and where masses could get access to information.[430]

Has the quality of 'filler' media induced a malaise across the public?

The first criterion for a healthy democracy is an educated public.

That is, a population which is educated in critical thinking, in seeing through fallacies and refusing to be sedated by dumbed-down platitudes.

Is there not a thirst for knowledge, understanding and intelligent conversation?
Have too many been content to just sit back and let the world flow by?
Have they given up the hope that they can make a difference?

The cutting edge comes when survival is on the line

When there is no food on the table, when the sky is no longer blue nor the sun shining, when the comforts that we take for granted have been taken away, when our phones and computers no longer work, when technology is not solving the problems as we expected, when the money that we thought we had has been taken away as plunder or scam, when we all wear masks in the smog, when someone is shooting at us ... and when no-one cares to help.

That will be the real wake-up call.

Why did we listen to the vested interests who said that Man is not affecting the climate?

Why did we assume that someone else would fix things?

In some parts of the world, these scenarios are already here. There are sixty-five million refugees or displaced people. That is about the population of France or twice the population of Saudi Arabia.

While politicians and the media peddle isolationist fears of how different cultures will make our world worse, should we not check our facts, isolate the fallacies and demand that the information is accurate?

Morality is not passive.

Isn't it about trying to do what is right, about insisting that what is done to us and in our name is right?

Isn't it about not turning away in the face of wrongdoing?

In democracies, we each have a say and we can influence outcomes – individually and collectively. Generally, changes of government in democracies reflect voters' wishes and they happen peacefully. That has to be a plus.

British wartime prime minister, Winston Churchill, made many famous quotes. But at the height of his political fame on 8 December 1944, he spelled out his view of the role of the ordinary voter, in the House of Commons:

'How is that word "democracy" to be interpreted? My idea of it is that the plain, humble, common man, just the ordinary man who keeps a wife and family, who goes off to fight for his country when it is in trouble, goes to the poll at the appropriate time, and puts his cross on the ballot paper

showing the candidate he wishes to be elected to Parliament—that he is the foundation of democracy. And it is also essential to this foundation that this man or woman should do this without fear, and without any form of intimidation or victimization. He marks his ballot paper in strict secrecy, and then elected representatives together decide what government, or even in times of stress, what form of government they wish to have in their country. If that is democracy, I salute it. I espouse it. I would work for it.' [431]

Perhaps the system just needs to work more effectively and efficiently to address the harder questions. (See Chapter 18)

THE MOST AVOIDED QUESTIONS

Learning never exhausts the mind
Leonardo da Vinci

Chapter 18

Are other alternatives to democracy clearly bad?

On 11 November 1947 in the House of Commons, former British Prime Minister, Winston Churchill said,

'Many forms of Government have been tried, and will be tried in this world of sin and woe. No one pretends that democracy is perfect or all-wise. Indeed, **it has been said** *that democracy is the worst form of Government, except for all those other forms that have been tried from time to time.'* [432]

There are many forms of government which are not democracies. They could, for example, be:
- a monarchy, which is ruled by one royal person.
- an oligarchy, which is ruled by a small number of people like an aristocracy or the military. Usually, in practice, the rulers are very wealthy. This system had its origins in ancient Greece where, for a time, they sought to appoint the best qualified people to run the country.
- a theocracy, where religious leaders govern the people and act as interpreters of God's will.
- a technocracy, where a number of specialists who are not politicians run the country. They might be scientists or technologists.[433]

Within those forms of government are ideologies which influence how the government might operate. **Ideologies are frameworks of thinking** – versions of world views as they relate to politics, economics and philosophy.[434]

For example, **Western democracies generally operate on a capitalist ideological model** which involves the notion of private ownership of businesses, free markets and trading – allowing the economic processes of money or capital to generate a profit and a good living standard.[435]

Critics of this model point out that it has generated a class system where the working people produce goods and services for wages or salary. The goods are then sold for a profit. The profit comes from the sale price being greater than the cost of production.[436]

The profits to the owner class are then invested in other ventures to give a further return. This investment self-generates competition and the need to keep investing and producing, to achieve more economic growth.

The benefits to the working people are much less than the benefits to the owner capitalists, who have taken the business risks. A small number of top capitalists can become very wealthy on the labour of many workers.

In the view of the critics, the motivation of the capitalist strategists is not to benefit society. It is based on using natural resources, technology and cheap labour to make wealth, mainly for the business owners and investment shareholders.

The system has been in place throughout the colonial era and has been reinforced in the minds of society by the institutions of education, religion and government. This has generated a culture that espouses that the only realistic way forward is by *economic growth*.[437]

A Philosophical Morality Challenge

Communism is another ideological approach in which all the businesses are owned by the state, ostensibly for the benefit of the public, who are those living in the classless society.

The ideology was based on the philosophical writings of Karl Marx and Friedrich Engels.[438] They produced a book called *'The Communist Manifesto'* in 1848, where they pointed out the weaknesses in the capitalist model and suggested a different way forward. Their position was that business decisions should made for the good of the people as a whole.[439]

Critics of this system point out that practical examples of communism, like the USSR ended up actually being ruled by an elite who controlled everything – in effect an oligarchy, or during Stalin's reign it would be better described as a dictatorship.[440] The Soviet Union never became a communist state in the way that Marx and Engels had described, although it used the terminology.

Other examples, such as China, also lost their way in creating a workers' state. Indeed, China has embraced many aspects of capitalism, in practice, since the economic reforms of 1978.[441] Today, the People's Republic of China is the second largest economy in the world but it has retained much of the discipline of an authoritarian state.

Actually, an important premise in Marx's view of the communist and socialist states was that the workers should have a say – a type of democracy in a sense.

In the USSR, China and Cuba, the governments lost touch with the needs of the ordinary people and that enabled powerful individuals to have an almost despotic rule. The voting system only really allowed the people to vote for members of the Communist Party. And it suited those in power to continue the charade.

Opponents of communism have used the worst excesses of these regimes to disparage the ideology completely. For example, in the

1950s at the height of the Cold War between the West and the Soviet Union, it was akin to being called a traitor to be denounced as a communist in western countries – and show trials were held the USA during the McCarthy era to identify traitors.[442]

Since that time, capitalists in the Western world seem to have claimed most ideological terms ending in 'ist' (except capitalist) to be derogatory. So, *socialist* and *communist* sympathisers became enemies of successful capitalist states. In more recent times, *fundamentalist* is an extremist follower of a religion. *Islamist* is an extreme fundamentalist who is using a peculiar interpretation of Islam to justify his/her actions, and a *populist* is someone who appeals to what the people are asking for – as distinct from what the leaders might think is best for the people.

Since the collapse of communism in the former Soviet Union, many privately-owned, Russia-based, multi-national companies have proliferated in the country – forming what may be classed as an oligarchy. In May 2004, the Russian edition of Forbes identified thirty-six business owners, each worth at least $1 billion.[443]

Just because there has been an expansion of negativity about ideologies that are different from capitalism, doesn't exclude them from having any merit at all.

It is more that their theoretical proposals have been gazumped by the elite powerbrokers who have garnered power for their own self-interest. There are those who currently argue that elitism is also the case in many capitalist countries, as demonstrated by the disparity of wealth (see Chapter 8).

Communalism is another system. It is a libertarian, socialist, political philosophy developed by Murray Bookchin[444] to complement his environmental ideas on social ecology.

It proposes that land and enterprises be placed in the custody of the citizens, in free assemblies. The maxim, *'From each according to his ability, to each according to his need'* is the guide for an economically rational society, guided by ecological standards, to replace the capitalist imperative of 'grow or die'.[445]

Communalism is also reflected in modern African thinking. In Africa, it is about structuring the developing society based on a collection of villages and their cultures. It is about the interrelatedness and inclusion happening together. It is also about shedding the constraints of colonial economics.[446]

Given the information presented here and in previous chapters,

Democracy, for all its faults, should at least give people a say in how they are governed. That shouldn't be a bad thing.

However, the reality of the system in democratic capitalist countries is that much of the political system is controlled by those wishing to retain the status quo – a governing political class, supported by a civil service bureaucracy. The control at the ballot box remains with the voting public but **'smoke and mirrors'**[447] create a persuasive illusion which tries to suggest that the process is much more democratic than it actually is. That elite approach is, in some ways, little different from the authoritarian systems.

Michael Schulson, in his 2014 article, argues the case for **random selection of representatives to government**, citing that if it was good enough for the Ancient Greeks it might be good enough for current houses of representation.

He argues that the United States House of Representatives is not representative of the people. It is 80 per cent white, old men. They have a median wealth of $900 million and a third of them have law degrees.[448]

Schulson points out that John Adams, who became the second president of the United States, wrote in 1776 that the general assembly *'should be, in exact miniature, a portrait of the people at large'*.

While that might be an idealistic thought and certainly not what happens in most democratic houses, let us hold onto John Adams' suggestion for a few moments.

Dr Alessandro Pluchino, and his colleagues at the University of Cantania in Italy, conducted research into how a randomly-selected, two-party assembly of five hundred people might make decisions. Their findings were that, in all cases studied, **the process of adding random legislators improved the performance of the parliament**. Specifically, there were more acts passed with social benefit.

'Most people think that democracy means elections,' they wrote. *'However ... in the first significant democratic experience, namely the Athenian democracy, elections worked side by side with random selection (sortition) and direct participation.'* [449]

Dr Pluchino and colleagues say that the drawbacks of a system dominated by political parties have been well documented. These include the tendency for politicians to follow a 'party line' and the tendency of groups to defend their interests.

Arguments in favour of random selection are that it can reduce corruption, prevent the dominance of a small group of politically active people, and ensure people of different incomes, races, religions and sex, are more fairly represented in parliament.

So, is the notion of representation by electorates set in stone for democracies?

Generally, politicians in lower houses are elected from a list of candidates within geographical areas, without **quotas or random selection**. There are some countries which reserve parliamentary places for specific groups – gender, religion, ethnicity (e.g. Cyprus, Fiji) – but they tend not to be the mainstream democratic countries. [450]

There can be some subtleties of quotas such as in Tasmania, Australia – proportional representation within electorates from a single transferrable vote[451] using the Hare-Clark system.[452] But, even in that example, parties limit the choice by preselecting candidates for election. And, because of their advertising profile, the party choice is usually elected. Occasionally, independents are chosen, particularly in the houses of review.

But, for minority groups or for a percentage of women to be elected, there is still no quota system in the major democracies of Europe and North America.

There are many counter arguments to having such a quota process, such as there needs to be a base level of education for the people who construct legislation or that women should be appointed on merit not on gender allocation.

Also, Sweden, without any quota for women in parliament, is a world leader in female participation with 43.6 per cent of seats taken by women in 2014.[453] This is a reflection of national approach to gender equality across the country. By comparison, the percentage of women in Canada's parliament in 2015 was 26 per cent.[454] In Australia, it was 29 per cent in the lower house in 2016.[455]

However, in many developing democracies of Africa, there **are** quotas for women representatives.

Dr Gretchen Bauer of the University of Delaware, notes that, since 2003, the use of electoral gender quotas has dramatically transformed national legislatures in Africa, with several countries having 30 per cent or more women in their houses of parliament. The initial countries were Rwanda, Burundi, Eritrea, Mozambique, Namibia, South Africa, Tanzania, Uganda and, a bit later, Angola. But they have been followed by Kenya, Lesotho and South Sudan, with many West African countries now considering the option.[456]

So, if countries can successfully use quotas for representation by women – changing the mindsets of generations – why not open the mind to other minority options as well? Or is the current electoral system too ingrained in the traditions of the former colonial-leadership lands?

Let us return to John Adams' suggestion of the house of assembly which reflects the population at large and Michael Schulson's argument for random selection.

In addition to quota systems and free elections, is there a rational argument to counter having parliaments formed, in some part, by random appointment from the general public – to produce 'a house of the people' which is more representative than the current practice? We do it consistently in many countries for juries in courts of law.

So, are other alternatives to democracy clearly bad?

From the evidence presented here, the democratic principle of everyone being able to have a free say in the government of their country should be a good thing.

However, the conventional structures that are used within democracies might well compromise that principle.

The system can be, and has been, 'gamed' or manipulated to retain the status quo.

Likewise, the ideologies which drive the elected governments can also have a bearing on the effectiveness of government. The impasse of aggressive delaying tactics from opposing ideologies may well be stymieing good government throughout many democracies.

Perhaps it is time to review the practices, even to the extent of questioning the universality of elections, as compared to a portion of random selection or quotas, to approach an actual representation of the population.

To break the deadlock, and to provide the leadership that is needed to address the significant challenges facing the world, it may well be time to revisit the unchallengeable tenets of modern democracies. Despite the denigration of other models of governance, there can be aspects of merit in several of them.

Could we try parts of other approaches?

To ignore options from oppositional ideologies would be a fallacy of false dichotomy, of ambiguity – **this is not an 'either one or the other' discussion.** There could be many useful inputs from other possibilities.

The moral question is:

Do we watch the dysfunction continue or do we choose to make things happen?

Part of the solution is to educate ourselves and to help others access learning, so that the bar of expectation for government performance is raised to a fully effective level.

The alternative to a peaceful growing awareness might be that those who have access to military force will choose to use it – as happened on a large scale in the 20th century.

And then, after all that pain and suffering, people still had to sit down in the aftermath to discuss how to move forward.

*When all is said and done,
there will be a lot more said than done.*

Aesop

Chapter 19

Whose rules are right in a global society? For example, refugees – humanity or someone else's problem?

When decision making is tense in democratic countries, elected representatives frequently polarise into talk of either hope or fear for the future.

So far, we have indicated that large parts of the world have different views on how their people and countries should be governed. Likewise, while there are certainly some similarities in views on human rights, they tend to diverge on human rights, of women in particular. Let us now consider refugees.

The situation of refugees is causing significant concern across the globe.
Sixty-five million displaced people is the population of a country like Britain.

The moral question is: how we should we deal with refugees?
The context appears to have changed since the aftermath of World War II. At that time, every country was aware of the enormous death and destruction which had happened over at least a five-year period.

Refugees were welcomed in many countries as the reconstruction of infrastructure, economies and governance occurred in the damaged areas.

But the population of the world at that time was 2.5 billion.[457]

There was space for the displaced to find areas of 'like people', where the rules of the land were compatible with their religions or values. Today, the world population is approaching 8 billion by 2025. That is a very different context.

There have been significant conflicts and natural disasters in many parts of the world over the past decade. That accumulation of threat has displaced people in the Middle East, Africa and Asia, who are fleeing war zones and famine … while some are just seeking a better life.

- People smugglers have taken criminal commercial advantage of desperate people. That has placed new pressures on countries in the Mediterranean, southern Asia and Australasia.
- In an attempt to prevent the trade in human misery, borders have been closed and the passengers in the trade have been demonised for their illegality and possible links to terrorism.
- While countries like Jordan, Lebanon, Turkey, Greece and Indonesia cater for hundreds of thousands in camps, others use isolated detention centres and razor-wire fences to deter potential refugees from choosing to follow.
- Furthermore, there is a political and media campaign of marginalising those who might be different or 'other', because of cultural background, religion or language.[458]

Refugees are being demonised in many countries. This creates division within the community. It generates controversy, media exposure and incites the fear of something largely unknown but potentially threatening. It also might appear to demonstrate that governments are taking strong action to protect their people from a threat.

It is not illegal to seek refuge in another land. It may be illegal to arrive without an approved visa or not to come through an approved migrant entry program.

It appears to serve a purpose of fear to imply that terrorists could possibly be among incoming refugees.

To illustrate, the term *Islamist* is being used to describe those members of Daech/ISIS who are claiming an extreme interpretation of Islam to justify why they invaded and tried to colonise parts of Iraq, Syria and northern Africa, using terrorism and a level of exceptional violence which is unusually ferocious for our current century.

That association is then being used to imply that *terrorist, refugee* and *Islam* might all be synonymous ... and that Sharia law might take over the country.

The **2016 Australian Census**[459] showed that:
- 'No religion' was the most common belief category at 30 per cent, having been at 22.3 per cent in 2011 and 19 per cent in 2006.[460]
- The religion of Islam is followed by 2.6 per cent of the Australian population – an increase from 2.2 per cent in 2011.
- Catholic followers dropped from 25.3 per cent in 2011 to 22.6 per cent in 2016.
- Christians, generally across all denominations, identify as 52 per cent of the Australian public,[461] compared to 64 per cent in 2006, 74 per cent in 1991 and 88 per cent in 1966.

That data hardly indicates a Muslim religion take-over.

Likewise, the Global Terrorism Database[462] demonstrates that present-day terror deaths, worldwide, are much less prevalent now than in the 1980s and 1990s, despite the media coverage, and that the attacks have predominantly been conducted by home-grown activists – **not refugees.**[463]

Despite many efforts by muftis and community leaders to denounce terrorists as a fringe group of gangsters and to explain the peaceful beliefs of the majority of Islamic religion followers, it has become a political tactic to marginalise whole communities as a result of the few.

What is the moral position? Is there a correct position?
There is no problem with sovereign countries subjecting refugees to identity and health checks, to minimise potential problems for the population generally. Most developed countries have some form of orderly migrant and refugee intake process, as well as border protection to prevent illegality and the import of biological threats.

The challenge comes through the scale of the refugee displacement. Australia's population in the 2016 census was 24 million. There are 65 million displaced people seeking refuge in the world.

So an association with Islam has become a current target for potential exclusion, in some countries. Opponents of the religion present the worst case scenarios as illustrations of the whole. This is a fallacy of composition – using a small number to imply the total.[464]

For example, within Sharia law there are references to the ancient death sentences of stoning. There are also references to the unacceptability of homosexuality.

In addition, there have been significant murders and terrorist activities around the world that have attributed their motivation to association with ISIS or Allah. So, the much-publicised atrocities have been taken to equate these incidents to Sharia and to the calls for banning or marginalising **all** Muslims on that basis.

The laws of democratic Western countries are determined by their parliaments or congresses – not by theology, nor Sharia in particular.

To demonstrate:
- Within the Catholic religion, canon law[465] has existed for centuries. It is not the law in Western countries. It has no jurisdiction in civil law. It administers the operation of the churches. If there have been any influences of canon law which may be reflected in the laws of Western lands over the centuries, they have been debated by elected representatives before being adopted as appropriate for their time and context.
- Within Australian Aboriginal communities, there is traditional community law which is used to sort out some community disputes.[466] It is not the law of Australia, either. Australian common law takes precedence.
- The vast majority of practising Muslims take Sharia (literally 'a path to a watering place')[467] as the set of guidelines for religious observance. Sharia is a collection of written texts that cover all aspects of Muslim life, in a similar way that Christians follow the general principles and values of the Bible rather than adopting some of the recorded attitudes of many centuries before (which also often included stoning to death[468]).

According to Dr Jan Ali, a lecturer at Western Sydney University, *'There is no country in the world that actually completely depends on Sharia. That's why we don't have Islamic countries, we have Muslim countries.'*[469]

Dr Ali says that if there is a conflict between Australian laws and Sharia, then Australia's laws do prevail. For example, Sharia allows Muslim men to have up to four wives. That apparently occurs in some countries but, in Australia, it can only be one wife. That is Australian law.

The next tactic is to **use terminology to divide Muslims**. In naïve efforts to show that most of the followers of Islam are not extremists, the terminology of appeasing politicians and commentators refers to that majority as 'moderate' Muslims.

Safraz Manzoor, in his 2015 UK *Guardian* article,[470] argues against that labelling of ordinary Muslims.

His interviewees rejected being called 'moderates' because they believe that they are the ones who are actually following their religion appropriately, including dressing in a particular way. To them, that is Islam.

Their argument is that the violent extremists have nothing at all to do with the religion of Islam (the extremists are using their alleged association in a criminal way).

They suggest that the use of divisive labels are alienating and that they come from a lack of understanding of the Muslim faith.

Manzoor quotes a BBC survey as indicating 95 per cent of Muslims (in Britain) freely claim loyalty to Britain and deplore the Paris atrocities at the *Charlie Hebdo* offices.

Asiyo Rodrigo, in her 2016 article[471] on what Shari'ah (her spelling) means to her, highlights how Sharia can guide her Australian life in a very positive manner. In part, she writes:

'For me, Shari'ah is not a set of specific laws but an overarching framework of divine principles through which I base certain decisions about my life. It is Shari'ah that informs my choice to comply with the laws of my country, even if I may be vocal about certain policies that are unfair.'

Hers is a much longer story about how many peaceful Muslims, like her and her family, have lived and worked in Australia without sensation for over a century. She adds:

'To watch my nation sink deeper into sensationalist scaremongering, using cherry-picked quotes found online to tar my beliefs, is draining. As Muslim women, we are already tired of constantly clarifying that we can in fact think for ourselves, and that Muslims have had a positive presence in Australia since the 19th century.'

In essence, Sharia is not the law of Australia – nor is canon law, nor traditional Aboriginal law.

A Philosophical Morality Challenge

Rodrigo continues:

'For ordinary Muslims like myself, turning the Australian legal system into one like Saudi Arabia's could not be further from the agenda. Rather, Islam guides to understand that the higher self does not require dominion over others, and that the state of the world is a reflection of the state of our hearts. In that sense, your Muslim neighbours and colleagues share the same challenge.'

Morally, as long as people are good citizens, they should not be denigrated because of their faith, their occupations, their dress or their accents. Indeed, their virtues should be celebrated.

If you read Chapter 14 again, you will note that attitudes to superiority and inferiority have little basis – except to marginalise, humiliate and incite jingoism, which is a type of behaviour that most Australians would decry if it happened to vilify them.

Esteemed Australian children's book author, Mem Fox, in February 2017, described feeling insulted and humiliated by aggressive border protection officials at Los Angeles airport, as part of a roomful of people who were all being detained for two hours to check visas.

Fox had been en route to address a conference in Milwaukee, with an Australian passport and a perfectly valid visa.[472] She had visited the United States many times before, without incident, in her roles as guest speaker at writers' conferences. But, suddenly, she was drawn into what she felt to be a demeaning situation as a result of a culture of negativism being promoted by people in leadership positions.

As Fox saw it, that is the climate of intimidation and fear when a little information is used to scare populations.

In a previous era, it was Judaism that was being isolated and denounced. History records how that turned out in the 20th century, as well as in times before.

With respect to refugees: **Is the morality of how people can be treated to be determined by worst case scenarios – effectively judging everyone by the lowest common denominator?**

If government spokespeople and the media were to present a more normal or common scenario, rather than inflated sensations, would that produce a more measured approach to visitors or people who appear to be 'others'?

Sixty-five million refugees is an enormous problem. As indicated in an earlier chapter, to some extent, parents are responsible for the children they bring into the world. Not all the displaced people are fleeing war zones.

It could be a valid line of dismissive argument for some nations to present that refugees are not the problem of potential receiving countries – the receiving countries did not create the situation.

However, the 1951 UN Refugee Convention[473] places a moral and 'legal' obligation on signatory nations to deal with refugees in a non-discriminatory manner and not to impose penalties on them, whether or not they entered illegally (Article 31).

The balance in these sorts of debate is to ensure that the premises for argument are based in fact rather than fallacy or emotional fear-mongering.

However, no matter what the persuasions are, at the end of the debating process, **the number facts don't change.** After all the proposed solutions or suggestions to *'go back where you came from'*, there are still sixty-five million people seeking a place to be, to live, to belong. That is the reality.

From a proactive general stance, education to slow the global birth rate must be a priority, particularly in areas which are subject to such movements of displaced people. (See Chapter 5)

China has successfully slowed the fertility rate and changed the attitudes to the size of families. It was a harsh imposition from the top;

a hard decision for good motives and they should be given credit for the achievement of lasting beneficial outcomes, in a macro sense.

However, once children have been born, the responsibility for their welfare rests primarily with the parents. But then, also, with the rest of us who share *the lifeboat* of the planet.

Don't we all have to make moral decisions?

What should the moral position be on dealing with displaced people? What is the right position for this time and context?
There is the provision for sovereign countries to restrict the entry of visitors, through the use of visas.

In countries that are dealing with mass influxes of displaced people in refugee camps, the burden of support should require assistance from other nations, particularly when there is such a disparity of wealth across the world.

While writers like Garrett Hardin[474] would disagree with that approach and argue that families need to take responsibility for their own plight, there is sufficient humanitarian spirit in the world to offer help.

For example, Canada remains committed to take 40,000 refugees in 2017, including 25,000 Syrians. Within the Canadian population, 75 per cent support the move with 25 per cent concerned at how successful it may be and urging for a stay on the intake.[475]

However, not all of the 65 million displaced people can be easily absorbed into the space of other nations. If it is to be an assimilation, rather than a welfare invasion, it needs resources in the accepting countries to assist with language, shelter and work.

In many of those receiving countries, there are already growing unemployment rates, so the ability to welcome newcomers will probably depend on new employment prospects, such as large infrastructure projects.

> *There needs to be a global cultural change in attitude towards people who are seen as 'other' or 'someone else's problem'.*

The argument that refugees are someone else's problem works to an extent ... but only for as long as history is not taken into account. The wealth disparity and environmental degradation is a product of multiple generations fashioning and transforming the global social and physical environment into the one in which we all currently live. **We are all part of the present scene.**

If the justification for 'someone else's problem' is that some have won the lottery of life and others haven't, then we are back to reassessing the moral positions on:
- 'all life being valued'
- the human rights espoused in the UDHR and the Cairo Declaration

and we are advocating 'hands-off' solutions which inevitably must lead to the mass deaths of the alienated or the disadvantaged.

That is a very different slant on morality being a product of time and context. That approach means that 'those who have' can do as they choose and ignore the plight of others ... while 'those who have not' can perish.

Is that a sound moral position?

The era of self-interest needs to phase out. There are very good vibes that people can gain from giving and sharing rather than collecting. **Greed and domination don't have to be the driving forces of life on Earth.**

The root causes, which allowed the disparity of wealth to develop, are still constantly being promoted through media, social institutions and political policies as the unchallengeable tenets of living in the 21st century. (Read again Chapters 8, 9 and 10.) That is not a sustainable recipe for long-term species survival. Spaceship Earth is one planet.

If there is only one lifeboat, there needs to be a logical, moral balance between sovereign security and humanity – not an easy challenge but one which needs to be faced, and certainly not avoided.

It would be naïve to think that Australia, for example, with a population of 24 million in 2016, could continue blithely into the foreseeable future with a projected annual intake of permanent migrants amounting to 190,000 (of whom only 3.2 per cent or 6,000 are likely to be resettled refugees, based on 2015/2016 data[476]).

Meanwhile, many hundreds of thousands struggle to survive in transit camps around the world and, in Indonesia alone, 14,000 refugees await their chance to be resettled.

The arithmetic of the pressure of displaced population, coupled to the apparent wealthy, average lifestyle of Australians and the space on the continent, would suggest that the same migration policy and political rhetoric cannot have an indefinite future.

When faced with actual situations on the ground, the morality of aspiration is not the same as the moral challenges of reality. Politics and ideology play a part.

While some countries have chosen to take an isolationist approach – supported by the opinion of many in their populations – **other countries have had no choice in accepting refugees.**

To some extent, they are the poorest countries:[477]

- **Turkey currently hosts 2.8 million refugees**, largely displaced from the conflicts around Syria and Iraq.
- **Pakistan has 1.2 million refugees** from Afghanistan and the Middle Eastern conflicts.

- **Iran** hosts **978,000 refugees**.
- Compared to the size of their countries and their economic capacity to assist, **Lebanon** at 1 million, plus **Jordan, South Sudan** and **Chad** carry the biggest burdens.
- 40 per cent of the countries in the top ten of refugee-hosting countries are in sub-Saharan Africa.[478]

Potential solutions are subject to their time, their context and the ability of governance to cope with the changing scenario.
- There are short-term challenges to render meaningful assistance to suffering people through a sense of common humanity, while cracking down on the criminal exploitation of vulnerable refugees, by deed or word.
- Further challenges would be to **stop the wars, intimidation and terrorist activities** which create the instability to displace the people in the first place. That is a function of power, space, population pressure on resources, and the greed that we have touched on in previous chapters.

The longer-term challenges return to the earlier discussions of:
- the disparity of wealth and obsolete economic models
- the loss of jobs to automation
- control of exponential population growth
- self-interest
- entitlement to privilege
- the inability of democratic governments to get beyond the theatre of debate to achieve outcomes
- the intransigence of non-democratic governments to assist in any meaningful way.

It is dangerous to be right in matters on which the established authorities are wrong

Voltaire, in the reign of Louis XIV

Chapter 20

Should the next generation have life better than we have had?

This is the 'better life' fallacy. Parents often want the future world of their children to be an improvement on the challenges that previous generations had to work through. **There is a flaw in that aspiration.**

Part of the reason that many parents have been successful is because they had to battle through hard times, to get knocked over in the disasters of life and to pick themselves up and start again.

It is natural for a parent to want the children not to suffer difficult times, to learn lessons from their parents on how to avoid hardship – but in the process …

> *The children are possibly missing out on what they need most; resilience and persistence.*

History is full of successful business people bequeathing their assets to the next generation, only for the businesses to fail and for the assets to be lost.[479] The missing ingredients of passion for the work, the adaptable smarts and the toughness to battle on through adversity were not necessarily passed on.

Before the exponential population expansion after World War II and the easier access to vehicular transport, children used to walk, run or cycle to school. Today, there is a line-up of cars and SUVs outside many urban schools in developed lands, as children are dropped off and picked up by parents – so that the young ones will come to no harm.

Indeed, there are laws in some countries (such as Australia) about not leaving children under the age of twelve without reasonable supervision. That could include walking to school or being left at home – the judgement would be in the hands of a court if something were to go wrong, after considering the circumstances.[480]

The 'cotton wool' children[481] are protected and molly-coddled by 'helicopter parents'[482] so that life will be pleasant and they won't have to experience setbacks.

However, the world after school is rarely so accommodating. Young people need the verve and toughness to bounce back after the inevitable disappointments.

Many of the earlier chapters in this book have emphasised **the importance of education** in helping to reshape the challenges facing most of the world's countries. Not only can secondary education delay the need for teenagers to have children, particularly in many African and Asian countries, but it can also develop critical-thinking minds across the world.

However, education does not equate to schooling.

Schooling is only one part of how young people learn skills, expertise and attitudes. Family and community associations are major character developers for the youth. Persistence, resilience, empathy and a thirst for life-long learning are inculcated from family and peer groups … or not, if there has been no past emphasis on such skills.

Schooling is about training adolescents in the priorities that governments or religions believe to be important. That could range from the fundamental skills of reading, writing and calculating through to a more social agenda such as cultural priorities, health and sex awareness programs, handling relationships, team work, appreciating diversity, life survival skills, driver education and job applications.

Most countries have a prescribed base curriculum of language, mathematics, science, social science, technology, the arts and physical education. Within that broad curriculum, students could also be expected to develop sophisticated core skills such as analysing, explaining, comparing, contrasting, researching, extrapolating, hypothesising and justifying. **These are some of the attributes needed for critical thinking.**

The measurement of student progress at school is assessed by a range of examinations and assignments, against a series of anticipated standards.

Some sampling of student performance in basic skills is frequently compared against international performances. That sampling is used in the political arena to help form government policy and to inform public opinion as to the effectiveness of their schooling systems.

While the formalised schooling system is an important training process, it is also a social filter.

School results put students into grades or 'boxes' (see Chapter 11) which ostensibly select those who can go to university, those who can learn trades, those who can do community tasks and even those who don't fit the social mould.

The pressure on impressionable children to be successful in this filtering system can be a cause of significant stress in families.[483]

While there are many avenues to success for young people, it is not always perceived in that way as the adolescent 'branding' process proceeds. That can lead to social problems of alienation, particularly as government and media announcements portray successful people as high achievers. Add body image pressures through the Internet culture and social media to the mix, and young people can easily be confused in their life direction.

What should the moral position be?

The challenges of modern society are complex and the interrelationships can rarely be reduced to the simplistic commentary that features on conventional media or government talking points.

Resilience is a key character trait for survival.

Part of that toughness is the understanding that it is alright to fail and to carry on. That message needs to form a greater part of the social commentary – because that is what life is actually about,[484] not the aspirational perfectionist ideal of advertisers or spin merchants or 'happy-ever-after' movies.

People, young people in particular, need a sense of belonging and worth to lead healthy lives. Without that, they will seek other ways of gaining their self-esteem or perhaps retreat into substance abuse to forget it all.

The moral position, as a society, should be to recognise the fallacies for what they are. The adult role should be to help children and adolescents to understand and to not accept the waves of sales pitches that proliferate in modern society.

Australian journalist, Elizabeth Farrelly, in a 2017 opinion piece[485] highlights some of the above challenges:

'Our hyper competitive schooling system militates against a better world by entrenching inequality, wasting talent, destroying the humanities and giving the false impression that the point and purpose of education is to increase earning capacity.'

Society is full of inequalities and disenchantments. Not all share in the success or prosperity – as the disparity of wealth illustrates.

Even those who are lucky enough to be born into a free, developed country or have inherited family resources or had the time to engage in fun activities ... even they are frequently confused and disoriented by the meaning of life.

Mental health referrals and sessions with psychologists are more common amongst the privileged than they are with those battling through the survival challenges of life.[486]

The late comedian, Robin Williams, said that 'Cocaine addiction is God's way of telling you you're making too much money'.[487]

At the other end of the wealth scale, petrol sniffing and alcohol abuse amongst young people are major problems in communities where the youth see no relevance or way forward from their lot in life. It happens from Cambodia to Nepal to Nicaragua to Australia.[488]

> ***The moral position must be to recognise that these major social problems exist. They are symptoms of the catalogue of challenges which are often the most avoided questions of society.***

Inequity, lack of opportunity and a continuation of 'same old, same old' are unlikely to resolve the dilemmas – nor is there much assistance from the stalemate of government decision-making processes, despite the constant rhetoric.

> ***Political diversity should <u>energise</u> the drive to achieve policy outcomes – not stifle them by oppositional theatre or a handwringing lack of practical leadership.***

To return to the question of, *Should the next generation have life better than we have had?*

Probably it is a natural human response to have a sense of hope, of optimism for the future, a belief that things can be achieved.

History records many examples of people battling through difficulties to reach success. Narratives and legends record such achievements. The birth of children encourages the hope for new and successful lives as part of the natural succession of life. Clearly, parents should want the best for their offspring.

The alternative is the pessimistic view that we'll all be ruined.[489]

Yet, that parental aspiration might well mean that they are rearing a generation who could be less able than their parents to have a better life. The global changes, already discussed in these chapters, compound the difficulties as the population increases, resources deplete and competition for space continues.

A function of the global pressure has been to increase community regulation to meet the moral expectations of human rights, workplace safety and business operation. That, in turn, increases operational costs of business and reduces the ability to create work for a growing number of substantially unemployed.

Let us use as another example – **the myth of the 'must have' university education.**

High-quality university education can be a great asset for meritorious undergraduates and postgraduates who are developing high-level tertiary learning and researching skills. Social prioritising of an exposure to this level of thinking and awareness is an 'infrastructure' investment in the future potential of a nation's young people.

There is, however, another side – the sales pitch.

In the United States and many other developed countries, universities have to charge fees for their courses – they are businesses. Students, who don't have the family resources to pay upfront, are encouraged to take out student loans using the rationale that, **on average**, graduates will get better paying jobs and be able to easily pay back such borrowings.[490] That myth applies in other countries such as the UK and Australia.[491]

The bubble of the fallacy comes from the framing of the sales pitch.

An average means that while half the graduates may earn above that mean figure, the other half will be below. Not only will that bottom half earn less than the sales pitch suggests but there may not even be jobs for them at all – yet they will still have their substantial degree debts to repay.

Surely, there is a lack of ethical practice in those who peddle such non-guaranteed deals to impressionable teenagers.

Finally, let us consider: **what makes us assume that the next generation should have life better?**

Does it come from the waves of social persuasion about growth – economic growth, in particular?

Self-help books pledge access to wealth and happiness. Silver-tongued economic commentators and political treasurers gush their single-message mantras that growth is the only solution to the national and global lifestyle problems.

It is like the irresistible call of the Sirens in Greek mythology,[492] beckoning and enticing sailors towards them with false promise, when in actuality they will crash onto the rocks.

Does it come from years of experiencing a steady progression in lifestyle in many developed countries since the 1950s and 1960s?

This is more fuel to suggest that the economic commentators must be right in promoting their way forward – and that they have been, certainly for some people, in recent decades. But that path may well be a progression of depletion that is approaching an end.

Or does it come from a belief system that emphasises hope – that things will always get better or that people will be able to afford more?

Sadly, while hope is a salve for the worriers – that someone else will solve the problem – hope is not a strategy. At some stage, humans have to consciously either approve or change their direction.

There is an alternative approach to that thought process.

Could it be that we might be content with sufficiency?

That we could lead happy fulfilling lives, with a bit of routine maintenance, to keep our comfortable lifestyle where it is – **without endless growth.**

That is heresy to the current economists and politicians but sustainable living is a rational solution to many of the ills facing the world.

Could we make it our moral priority to help others?

If everyone looked after others, then other people, by the definition, would be looking out for you.

Being kind to others and sharing – isn't that what a family and a society is all about?

The positive focus on assisting others would take the focus away from self interest. That team work is a characteristic of communities that need to co-operate for survival and to make their moral decisions on behalf of the wider group – **to not be isolated islands in a sea of urban anonymity.**

Being content with sufficiency means that there is more to share with others.

Or …

Have we forgotten the lessons of history, that our material possessions can be gone tomorrow and we would go from a position of self-reliant comfort to being dependent on the kindness of others?

In the 1930s in Europe and later in the western Soviet bloc, **Jewish people** were isolated in the community, then all their possessions were taken.[493] They were moved into ghettos and then internment camps. For six million of them, they were then killed during the Nazi occupation in World War II.[494] They had been wealthy business people or professionals such as doctors, lawyers, teachers and academics. They had been tradespeople, mothers, fathers, grandparents and children. It made no difference ... and it all happened relatively quickly over less than a decade. They lost everything, including their lives.

In 2008, the **Global Financial Crisis** (GFC) was the largest financial collapse since the Great Depression of the 1920s. The Wall Street Journal estimated the losses to be $15 trillion USD.[495] Millionaires lost their millions, ordinary people lost homes, their employment and life savings. The effect was worldwide.

Some of the speculators and regulators went to jail but the investors' money – plus any illusory valuations within Ponzi schemes[496] – was gone.

It happened fast. Why?

Luci Ellis of the Reserve Bank of Australia noted:[497]

'Perhaps the most basic underlying driver of the crisis was the inherent cycle of human psychology around risk perceptions. When times are good, perceptions of risk diminish. People start to convince themselves that the good times will go on forever.'

Isn't that exactly the position we are in now – expecting that the good times will go on forever?

Yet, during the GFC, comfortable lifestyles evaporated and **formerly successful people were suddenly living on the edge.**

Currently, in the USA, there are 1.5 million **homeless people**, using shelters or sleeping rough.[498] A quarter of them are children.

In Australia, at the last census, 105,000 people were experiencing homelessness each night.[499]

In Canada, it is estimated that there is a core of 200,000 people homeless or one per cent of the population without the comfort of a home.[500]

These are but three of the more successful economies in the world (who publish homeless statistics).

By that measure, there is no certainty that what we now have will be retained indefinitely.

By what logic do we think that the next generation should have it better? Is it merely based on hope, from the context of our upbringing?

Contexts can change, not through any fault of our own. As illustrated, we can't always control how things will pan out in the future.

We also had no choice in when we were born, or to whom, or where.

- If you are **Rohingya in Myanmar**, you are being persecuted for being born as the person that you are.[501]
- Likewise, if you were born with the **Yasidis in Iraq** when the ISIS terrorists invaded, you were facing potential genocide … and many of your people were killed or taken captive.[502]
- If you were born to **Dinka parents in South Sudan**, where internal warfare still rages, your best prospect is a refugee camp in Uganda or Kenya.[503]

And these examples are without visiting the more renowned conflicts which are creating the major refugee movements.

If you are one of the displaced people around the world, your only hope is that some nation, *the lifeboat*, will take you on board and help you. The alternative is more of the same or worse.

In democratic countries around the world, it seems from recent voting patterns that a majority of disenchanted voters no longer believe that things will get better, under their current governance. They are voting against anything that is current practice – the status quo. In the USA, Australia and the UK, there have been large swings against the current government practices and policies.

Uncertainty is the new norm.

In countries under totalitarian rule, there is no protest allowed and no prospect of improvement for the majority. The people must adapt to what is happening or revolt. And revolt for them likely means a suicidal resistance against massive military power, so successful revolution won't come any time soon.

Faced with this, how are people in developed countries responding? Many are closing the borders and retreating into nationalist shells.

So, what is the moral solution?

Perhaps those *who have*, need to taste the survival experience of those *who have not*, which is causing so many to flee.

To wish war or loss of lifestyle on others is hardly a good moral choice – but there does need to be a cultural change; an attitude of understanding that we are on a finite path, a relic of earlier colonial ages. There are avoided questions to be asked and answered.

Some truth needs to be spoken and heard by those who make the major social decisions.

Obscene wealth in the face of abject poverty is surely not what is seen to be right in a moral society.

The challenge is **not unsolvable** but it is **complex** and **it will take time**.

- The approach is not about self-interest but it is about the interest of the survival of the species, long term.

- It will involve a global cultural change to accept that sufficiency, rather than always being greedy for more, is a practical step along the way.
- It will require a change in attitude to continued economic expansion which relies on resource depletion – and to replace it gradually with sustainable models of sufficiency.
- It will require restraint in the number of children being born.
- It will require meaningful employment/activity to engage people in a valued contribution to social life.
- It will require leadership of the type that sometimes emerges in eras of extreme hardship, like world wars – a wake-up call, a willingness to sacrifice some things in order to get wider outcomes on the path to sustainable recovery.

None of that is easy … but it is logical.

It always seems impossible until it is done

A likely alternative to a measured program of development that can work towards sustainable sufficiency over time … is that people will eventually go to war over land, over fresh water and resources. **That is the lesson of history.** That was a driver in the last world war – living space[504] and the co-prosperity sphere.[505] In the aftermath, when the guns are silent, people will still have to sit down to resolve the way forward with whatever is left.

In the words of General Douglas Macarthur at the surrender of Japan in Tokyo Bay on 2 September 1945: *'We are gathered here, representatives of the major warring powers – to conclude a solemn agreement whereby peace may be restored. The issues involving divergent ideals and ideologies have been determined on the battlefields of the world.'*[506]

Is that the best process we can come up with to resolve questions of right and wrong?

The hope for the future generation is not that they might have it better than we have had it.

Rather, it is that we don't want them to have to revisit the lessons of history.

We want them to be content with enjoying the planet, society and family.

That can happen for many future generations, if we don't avoid the difficult questions in this generation.

THE MOST AVOIDED QUESTIONS

If you think too long on the next step,
you will end up in life standing on one leg
Chinese proverb

Chapter 21

The conclusion – Now, how do you think moral decisions are made? The way forward? ... and when?

Having read the previous twenty chapters and checked the referenced sources in the end notes, *how do you now think moral decisions are made?*
Are they a product of their time and context?
Are some moral attitudes being retained because of tradition, entrenching them in custom and culture?

These chapters have demonstrated that ostensibly sensible people can view the same moral dilemmas from very different perspectives. That does not make them either wrong or right, in an absolute sense ... just different, in terms of their cultural context, their own value systems. In Shakespeare's words, *'There is nothing either good or bad, but thinking makes it so.'* Hamlet. Act 2 Scene 2.

Ideally ...

> ***Moral education should be about parents and the community enabling young people to become self-controlled, critical-thinking adults who have sufficient autonomy to respond to the challenges of life in a socially responsible manner.***

Perhaps what that means is that there could, and should, be a tolerance of 'other' ways and an appreciation of diverse thinking styles, rather than a one-size-fits-all, polarising approach to world morality.

- While the United Nations has a significant role to play in clarifying, praising and condemning the actions of others, it is not at the moment the absolute arbitrator of right and wrong.
- Neither should, or do, the many denominations of religions dictate for all, from their particular beliefs.
- The history of man's existence in the world would suggest that there will be dominant cultures and attitudes for periods of time. They will rise and fall ... or be overthrown by more dominant waves. Views on morality tend to follow the context of their time and context.

The cutting edge exists when there is no physical space for escape, for people's cultures to be divergent from a norm or to be free from one group's activities upsetting the survival conditions for others.

That is where morality, humanity and pragmatism meet from contrasting viewpoints – and the conflict of views and lifestyles can result.

We can ask some fundamental morality questions at this point.

As the population of the world approaches 8 billion and the disparity between rich and poor is widening ... **are those in power flexing their military muscles so that they can retain, or gain, their dominance?** That would be the imposition of one view of morality over an alternative, or a range of alternatives.

There are certainly many recent, overt indicators of brinkmanship or displays of military power flexing (e.g. Russian support in Crimea, eastern Ukraine and Syria, Turkish conflict with Kurdish separatists, Chinese claims for disputed islands in the South China Sea,

US-Coalition support of Iraqi Army efforts to remove Daech from its territories, Saudi Arabia and US incursions into Yemen, North Korean weapons testing over the Sea of Japan, US punitive missile strikes against Syrian gas attacks).

In addition, there are many more subtle indicators of behind-the-scenes posturing for additional territories or influence, particularly in the Middle East, the Baltic, eastern Asia and the Balkans.

Can the collective will of powerful nations sit in judgement on others with respect to 'crimes against humanity' or even 'crimes of political manipulation'?[507]

The current United Nations Security Council has five permanent members (United States of America, China, Russia, France and the United Kingdom) which reflect the preferred power perceptions after World War II.[508] Each of those countries has the power to veto any substantive or draft resolutions.

While that system was designed to limit minority or impulsive actions, critics would argue that it is undemocratic or unrepresentative and that it has been the main cause for inaction over 'crimes against humanity' or war crimes. The vested interests of 'the Big Five' tend to protect themselves or their allies.

Among the last few UN vetoes have been:
- Russia vetoing Aleppo bombing in Syria (2016)
- Russia vetoing a criminal investigation into the shooting down of the MH17 civilian aircraft over Ukraine (2015)
- Russia, with China, vetoing a UN condemnation of Syria (2014)
- The USA vetoing a resolution condemning Israeli settlements in the West Bank (2011)
- The USA, UK and France vetoing a condemnation of the USA invading Panama (1989).

Politics makes a fine art out of fallacy use, of using 'thin end of the wedge' and oppositional-extreme examples. The mainstream media exacerbates the sensationalism by reporting and presenting such statements as newsworthy information rather than untested opinion or provocations. It is always a matter of conjecture as to whether or not the media outlets are reporting the news or pushing particular viewpoints, with a range of motivations. Who decides what is 'news'?

The hurly-burly of politics should be distinguished from diplomacy, which actually looks for common ground, with some respect and grace, in the form of a mediation, a resolution, a positive outcome – without the grandstanding.

Current society has evolved to promote self-interest as a laudable goal for many activities – but that is probably not the best approach for human survival. If the end result is just a few formerly-rich families surviving on the planet, that is not a good recipe for successful reproduction. Indeed, it is a recipe for inbreeding regression.

How did we become so brainwashed?

Education is a key circuit breaker to the impasse – that is, critical thinking and the skills of respectful discussion.

That is not the same as the schooling of adolescents in their particular culture (beliefs, norms) nor the mindless indoctrination into someone's way forward.

There is a place to imbibe the mores of one's culture but probably not where it involves the exclusion of every other culture on the planet. Education is about accessing multiple frames of reference and being able to give a critical appraisal of information.

The vast majority of people can ask the question, **'Why is it so?'**

They have the ability to seek explanations and justifications that don't just naturally revert to attributing challenges to a deity's mysterious will. Most adults can accept that there are things that we don't know or can't yet explain. **It is the journey, towards trying to understand, that is exciting and fulfilling.**

The scientific method emphasises the certainty of doubt. That is why scientists are constantly hypothesising and testing conclusions. That approach does not sit well with people who feel they already know the truth, without the testable evidence. **It is important to learn the skills of reasoning from an early age – to question in a mannerly fashion, to challenge ideas.**

Is tolerance of other ideas a better approach than self-righteousness?

If morality is about making wise social choices, based on evidence and reasoning, then a consideration of a range of views is likely to be a rational way to sorting out the best moral way forward. That is a very different approach from a non-selective blind belief in 'one right answer'.

The evidence in these chapters suggests that *truth* and *right* are not absolutes. There can be interpretations of 'rightness' depending on the context of the changing times and the understandings from upbringings. Comparative ideas about moral dilemmas need to be proposed, considered, challenged and tested for their time and context.

Furthermore, a 'right answer' from one era is not necessarily the best moral solution for another situation and time – no matter how we might pretend that using statements from belief doctrines or past practice is the only correct value system. Every moral position should be examined for appropriateness to its context and time.

By all means, people should feel free to believe what they choose or to follow the religion of their choice. It may be that they say, 'If I believe it, then it is my reality. Therefore, it is real'. That may be enough for them to have peace in their belief. But, if that belief is used to affect others, they should also have some rationale, some logic, for developing a particular understanding – a reasoning process that others could also check and accept. It is possible that the appreciation of the facts may not be as robust as they had assumed. That is the certainty of doubt.

> ***Intelligent people can change their views if tested facts support that change.***

It is probably important to respect another person's right to think differently from you – **people, even friends, can disagree** – but, you **should** also feel sufficiently empowered to challenge any self-righteous viewpoints, whether that righteousness be from a religious, economic or ideological certainty. **That is especially important when the views might influence the laws of the land.**

No doubt, the convinced will use circular arguments that always come back to variations on 'That is the way it has always been' or the last bastion argument of the closed mind, 'If you can't explain the complexities of everything, I'll believe what I choose'. That is the old ambiguity of scope – a fallacious premise. Or the 'ad hominem' technique … what would **you** know about anything? They are using distracters to avoid having to think through uncomfortable ideas … or to protect themselves from having their contented lifestyle threatened.

By challenging their thinking, you will perhaps sow the seeds of doubt into their world of definiteness, and let them know that you understand that **it is alright to question**, even if you don't have all the answers.

Use the lessons of history to lay out an argument rationally –

> ***a number of valid, evidence-based premises leading to a logical conclusion without the use of distracting fallacies or resorting to untestable dogma.***

Undoubtedly, there is a comfort in being able to attribute the unexplainable to some other being and, we might all agree, that it will allow people to get on with daily routines without needing to struggle with deep philosophical concepts.

There is a place for spirituality in people's lives – that sense of wonder at the immensity of the universe through to the intricate beauty of a lily in the field. But a sense of spirituality does not necessarily equate to following a particular belief doctrine. Rather, awe at the complexity and beauty of the world is a place for pondering, questioning, learning – and being safe to do so without ridicule, abuse or fear of reprisal.

Likewise, **an understanding of the balance in the natural ecosystems** can come from simple experiments with profound meanings behind them. Such science can be conducted in a normal home.

- Try extracting the DNA string from a kiwi fruit in your kitchen[509]
- Show the process of osmosis with a simple cucumber experiment.[510]

The experimentation is simple – child's play – but the implications are immensely significant for understanding so many profound learnings that flow from those simple tests. For example, they help explain the function of our body systems and plant structures … right through to the genetic codes of life. And they are testable and repeatable. Just to start with simplicity leads to more questions being asked and more searching for answers for harder and harder queries.

Respect for others is a key concept in moving forward.

The conversation should be about the behaviour, not the person. Insults to people's dignity are rarely ever forgotten or forgiven.

It is easier to speak freely when one acknowledges the feelings of others. For example, it is less complicated to discuss the problems of the exponential adding to population, if it is not a shaming exercise. Not everyone has had a free choice in their circumstances.

Arguments need to be rational – not just opinion without testable premises – and to be delivered politely, with respect.

Life or death situations tend to focus the mind.

Context can affect how people view right and wrong.

If actual survival is the prime preferred outcome, the trappings of possessions become less relevant. **If the survival of a group is the priority, individual wants and needs lose their importance.**

In wartime, looking out for your mates and not letting them down, can produce extraordinary acts of selflessness – some of which are acknowledged by commendations for bravery.

Inherited or earned privilege is undoubtedly comfortable in the context of tranquil times but they are 'the emperor's clothes'.[511] Without them and the power that they imply, we are each no different from everyone else.

In Scotland, it is described in a common metaphor, 'We're all Jock Tamson's bairns', meaning that we are all the same, under the skin – no matter what the advantage or disadvantage.[512]

The homeless and destitute people may not always have been poor. They may well have had a change in their fortunes, not of their own making.

For example, a natural disaster – such as a tropical cyclone, a volcanic eruption, an earthquake, a flood or a wild forest fire – can remove all the trappings of a comfortable life and change people's fortunes forever.

Also, some are born into circumstances of disadvantage … and have no choice in their life chances.

How would survival contexts affect how you might view right and wrong?

An understanding of human history is important for everyone to make reasoned decisions.

Even allowing for variations in the interpretation of history, the general pattern shows enough of unchecked human behaviour to inform the present generations of the likely potential outcomes. It would be foolish to follow the same path and to expect a different result.

History can tell us about the strong invading the weak; and about which social checks and balances can hold back abusive behaviour. It can show us the considerable success stories, of how communities can work successfully together; and of the development of human knowledge in explaining the world around us.

History provides us with a record of evidence, of views, of attitudes, of reasoning that can help us understand ways to lead our own lives into the future. Studies in social anthropology have shown a need, throughout history, for cultural groups to explain life with beliefs in a range of deities.

However, with the accumulated knowledge of history, it is more likely that the moral challenges of our present times would benefit from a rational analysis (a trackable thought process) rather than evidence-free faith in some external power. Perhaps, there is a place for the occasional flash of intuition to progress thinking into new areas (particularly in research), but the rules of operating in society need a basis of understandable reasoning behind them.

One of the great tragedies in the history of war is that the sacrifice is often forced upon innocent people because they, and their leaders, didn't stand up to object when they could … to take a moral stance … if the likely solutions would mean giving up personal comforts or lifestyle.

And then it was too late.

The inexorable train of actions, so obvious to most who were not blinded by brainwashing, continued until the train went over the cliff.

Ponder the words of John Maxwell Edmonds, who wrote after the losses in World War I:

When you go home, tell them of us and say
For their tomorrow, we gave our today.[513]

We don't need to follow 'the calf path'.[514] We can see the futility of self-interested trajectories. We can see through fallacies. We don't need to be meekly herded. The inevitable is only inevitable if we allow greed, self-interest and madness to prosper as the correct way to operate in society.

Let us consider some concluding thoughts.

- **Most of the moral explanations and arguments in life are of the non-deductive type,** in that the evidence can suggest probable or possible courses of action – not definitive directions or policies, beyond **all** doubt.
- Deductive arguments – those that provide absolute conclusions and which would exclude all other possible deductions or possibilities – are rare in the world. That is particularly so when arguments deal with projections into the future.
- The statements (or premises) that make up logical arguments need to be valid (relevant to the final conclusion, rather than distractions or fallacies) and to be sound (true or verifiable).
- The most common rebuttal for arguments is to provide valid, checkable counter-examples which undermine the original premises. That is the process for civilised debate … and, indeed, for the scientific method.

Critical thinkers become skilled at exposing the weaknesses in arguments or evidence-free opinions. They do not accept fallacious or distracting tales, no matter how convincingly delivered.

That is the value of educating the mass of the people to reject 'rubbish' statements, particularly from people who should know better. (There is a non-deductive moral implication in that statement because those people probably know exactly what impact their outpourings might have. They are delivered for effect.)

But, those who choose to believe what they want to hear (confirmation bias) are like the subjects of hypnotism. **They are in a trance of self-belief – immune to alternative rational evidence.**

Perhaps, that is where the idea of brainwashing comes from; or the suggestion about the lack of free will. Or perhaps they choose to believe what they do because their newsfeeds are being controlled by social media algorithms to only expose particular subscribers to self-affirming viewpoints.[515] If that is so, they are not being exposed to alternative checkable perspectives.

Education is **one** answer to break that spell – to expose people to other views, to imagine walking in other people's shoes, and to absorb information from multiple frames of reference.

Being able to read is the key.

Having access to the volumes of knowledge in the world can open a mind to an Aladdin's cave of understanding.

The Scottish actor, Sean Connery, famously said that it was not his securing the role of James Bond in movies that was his big break – it was learning how to read at the age of five and finding public libraries.[516]

This concluding chapter does not pretend to provide the definitive answers to the most avoided questions. Rather, it provides a range of opposing observations that are checkable and which present themselves to be validated or challenged by replicable testing. That is the constant challenge of the scientific and logical methods – the certainty of doubt which can allow alert minds to infer the best available testable theories that might explain the mysteries of the world.

A tested hypothesis can confirm your observations – but, philosophically, it will be true only to the extent that it has not been proven false.

Tests can reject hypotheses when the experimental evidence does not support the propositions but they can't conclusively settle that they are true. As Karl Popper (1902–1994) said, in *The Logic of Scientific Discovery*: *'No matter how many instances of white swans we may have observed, this does not justify the conclusion that all swans are white.'*[517]

But ...

If a theory is not testable at all, then it belongs in the world of belief or fantasy.

The intent of this book is both to present a variety of considerations and to provoke the thought processes of readers.

Answers to these important moral questions will, for some people, require significant change and flexibility in long-held attitudes and thinking.

So, ask yourself:

Who should decide whether the survival of the species is more important than the rights of individuals to do as they please?

The captain of Spaceship Earth? The most powerful? The most rational? A majority of the international community in the United Nations? All of us, together? Each of us in our own sphere of influence?

Should societies continue their transformation of ecosystems for as long as they can, at the expense of other forms of life, until the systems collapse?

Nature will probably rectify the balance through some cataclysm (as has happened before in the geological history of the planet) but we might not be beneficiaries of that solution. (Read Chapter 10 again)

A Philosophical Morality Challenge

Would it be better to challenge certain assumptions of morality now?

This challenge is not to establish groupthink or consensus or even a majority. Rather, it is to lay out the projected consequences of our current practices, their history and their applicability for the world of the future. Let an educated public see the challenges without the smoke and mirrors of fallacies or the protection of privilege, tradition or status quo thinking.

Does our understanding of right and wrong, of morality, need to be informed by more than self-interest?

Change from the status quo will frequently be seen as a threat by those who have a comfortable or advantaged lifestyle ... those who stand to lose any part of that benefit. However, for those who feel disadvantaged or trapped by the status quo, change may well be seen as an absolute necessity for living in a fair world into the future.

We live in a world which, historically, has been largely shaped by the decisions, policies and legal systems of rich, white males ... and that is still the process in most of the countries and global corporations of the world. Look around!

So, *what priorities should guide our generally-accepted moral notions of right and wrong as we tackle the most avoided questions?*

Does morality need a more global social perspective?

The working hypothesis of this book is that every moral decision is a prisoner of its time and culture.

But sometimes, the moral decisions are frozen in the unchallengeable dogma of belief systems, or they become entrenched in laws of the land or they are accepted as inalienable truths enforced by international agreements, declarations, conventions or constitutions.

What is your view, now, after reading the alternative arguments and opinions?

THE MOST AVOIDED QUESTIONS

Where should the discussion go from here?

It would be naïve to think that solving the world's most avoided questions would have a simplistic single answer.

That would be akin to suggesting that the D-Day landings in 1944 would be as simple as landing a few troops on the Normandy beaches ... and World War II in Europe would be over.[518] But **we shouldn't be deterred by difficulty.**

In the history of wars, many people have foregone their personal rights and possessions to sacrifice in the interests of the greater good. *Was that a moral decision or pragmatism forced upon them?*

The solutions to the most avoided questions are nuanced and multi-faceted – onion layers of complexity, **but not unsolvable.** It needs the will to question, to see an objective beyond self. Some of the clues are in these pages. That is just the start.

We need a change in our cultural thinking. Cultural change has happened before.

In free societies, people:
- can inform themselves with the evidence rather than hearsay
- have the power to reject or accept the practices endorsed by governments
- have the freedom to protest
- can vote out governments and influence policy changes.

<u>You</u> can make change happen. If it is not to be <u>you,</u> then <u>who</u> ... ?

It is the first responsibility of every citizen to challenge authority
Benjamin Franklin

About the Author

Jim Reay is a former high school principal and senior public servant; later, a writer of short stories and mysteries, based in Brisbane, Australia.

Born a Scot, he brings a range of perspectives and critical thinking to his stories, as well as his love of history, learning and culture.

Now, with *The Most Avoided Questions*, he lays out a range of researched observations from multiple frames of reference with a view to provoking thinking, self-reflection and the development of an ability to see through fallacies.

www.jimreaywriter.net

If I have seen further, it is by standing on the shoulders of giants.
Sir Isaac Newton[519]

End Notes

Introduction

1 http://theconversation.com/you-say-morals-i-say-ethics-whats-the-difference-30913

2 Julius Sumner Miller (1909–1987) was an American doctor of physics who used television to make complex science principles understandable to children. http://www.mountainman.com.au/wyisitso.html

3 http://www.urbandictionary.com/define.php?term=alternative+truth

Chapter 1

4 Plato (died 348BCE) was a classical Greek philosopher who founded the first Academy in Athens, as a place of higher learning.

5 Socrates is often credited as being the founder of Western philosophy. He died in 399BCE at age 71.

6 Plato's *Republic*. Book 1. When Socrates is discussing Plato's meaning with Cephalus https://en.wikipedia.org/wiki/Republic_(Plato) https://books.google.com.au/books/about/Republic_Grube_Edition.html?id=5ZjRDTmOCMoC

7 https://en.wikipedia.org/wiki/Perjury

8 http://www.nj.com/politics/index.ssf/2016/07/rnc_2016_republicans_cheer_trumps_call_for_a_new_d.html

9 http://www.abc.net.au/news/2016-06-21/alberici-whipping-up-fear-to-sway-the-brexit-vote/7528104

10 http://www.politifact.com

11 http://www.todayifoundout.com/index.php/2010/02/the-difference-between-a-fact-and-a-factoid

12 Josef Goebbels was Reich Minister for Propaganda in Nazi Germany from 1933 until 1945.

13 https://www.ushmm.org/outreach/en/article.php?ModuleId=10007677

14 https://en.wikipedia.org/wiki/Freedom_of_speech_in_the_United_States

15 http://www.franksonnenbergonline.com/blog/honesty-the-plain-and-simple-truth

16 http://www.theepochtimes.com/n3/3913-chinese-character-for-harmony-he-%E5%92%8C/

17 http://www.mountvernon.org/digital-encyclopedia/article/cherry-tree-myth

18 Fletcher, Joseph. *Situation Ethics – The New Morality*, Westminster John Knox Press, Louisville London. 1966

19 https://en.wikipedia.org/wiki/Augustine_of_Hippo

20 http://theconversation.com/royal-commissions-how-do-they-work-10668

21 http://commissionwatch.com.au/what-is-a-royal-commission/

22 http://www.aph.gov.au/About_Parliament/Senate/Powers_practice_n_procedures/Brief_Guides_to_Senate_Procedure/No_20

23 https://en.wikipedia.org/wiki/Spin_(propaganda)

Chapter 2

24 http://www.history.com/topics/enlightenment

25 https://www.law.cornell.edu/wex/first_amendment

26 http://www.un.org/en/universal-declaration-human-rights

27 Voltaire (1694–1778) was a leading French philosopher during the Enlightenment.

28 http://www.goodreads.com/author/show/4585909.Evelyn_Beatrice_Hall

29 http://quoteinvestigator.com/2015/06/01/defend-say

30 Murray, Don. *"France even more fractured after the Charlie Hebdo rampage"*. CBC News. 8 January 2015.

31 http://www.dw.com/en/french-satire-mag-in-court-over-reprinted-mohammad-cartoons/a-2340200

32 A legacy of when those areas were part of Germany and the Germanic laws of that time, and they have never been revoked.

33 http://news.bbc.co.uk/2/hi/europe/6479673.stm

34 https://en.wikipedia.org/wiki/Law_on_the_Freedom_of_the_Press_of_29_July_1881

35 https://en.wikipedia.org/wiki/Charlie_Hebdo_shooting

36 http://www.bbc.com/news/blogs-trending-35108339

37 https://en.wikipedia.org/wiki/Muhammad

38 http://www.billionbibles.org/sharia/sharia-law.html As a legal system, Sharia Law can have a wide interpretation and exists in some form or other in twenty countries or more.

39 https://en.wikipedia.org/wiki/Inquisition
40 https://www.legislation.gov.au/Details/C2014C00014
41 http://www.abc.net.au/news/2016-09-01/what-is-section-18c-and-why-do-some-politicians-want-it-changed/7806240
42 https://en.wikipedia.org/wiki/Terra_nullius
43 http://treatyrepublic.net/content/brief-outline-mabo-judgement-and-its-implications
44 https://en.wikipedia.org/wiki/List_of_massacres_of_Indigenous_Australians
45 http://www.ramsskullpress.com/index.php/item/197-murri-on-a-mission-gunnan-gunnan
46 http://www.australianstogether.org.au/stories/detail/the-stolen-generations Hegarty, Ruth *Is that you, Ruthie?* University of Queensland Press 1999
47 https://www.jstor.org/stable/25746092?seq=1#page_scan_tab_contents
48 Hayes, Maurice. Access to Justice: in *Studies: An Irish Quarterly Review Vol. 99, No. 393, Power and Accountability in Ireland (Spring 2010), pp. 29–42*
49 https://en.wikipedia.org/wiki/Tort_law_in_Australia
50 http://www.bbc.com/news/world-europe-30835625
51 https://en.wikipedia.org/wiki/Human_rights_violations_during_the_Syrian_Civil_War
   https://www.nytimes.com/2017/04/05/world/middleeast/syria-bashar-al-assad-atrocities-civilian-deaths-gas-attack.html
52 http://www.iwm.org.uk/history/how-britain-hoped-to-avoid-war-with-germany-in-the-1930s

Chapter 3

53 http://www.aljazeera.com/news/2017/07/amnesty-saudi-stop-bloody-execution-spree-170726071519013.html
54 'Thou shalt not kill' is written in the Bible Old Testament in the Book of Exodus 20:13 and in Deuteronomy 5:17
55 This terminology of 'all life being sacred' appears in 19th century Protestant discourse, the Catholic encyclical of Rerum Novarum (1891) and, post World War II, in Catholic and evangelical moral theology
56 https://en.wikipedia.org/wiki/Code_of_Ur-Nammu
57 https://en.wikipedia.org/wiki/Quran
58 https://en.wikipedia.org/wiki/Assassins
59 *Thugthou gee (Thagi) (13th C. to ca. 1838).* Users.erols.com. Retrieved 2013-04-23.
60 https://en.wikipedia.org/wiki/Human_sacrifice_in_Aztec_culture#cite_

note-39

61 https://en.wikipedia.org/wiki/Thou_shalt_not_kill

62 https://en.wikipedia.org/wiki/Honor_killing

63 "Honor killing" under growing scrutiny in the U.S. – Crimesider". *CBS News. Retrieved 16 August 2013*

64 *Ruggi, Suzanne.* "Commodifying Honor in Female Sexuality: Honor Killings in Palestine". *Middle East Research and Information Project. Retrieved 8 February 2008.*

65 Chesler, Phyllis. Are Honor Killings Simply Domestic Violence?, *Middle East Quarterly,* Spring 2009, pp. 61–69

66 https://www.creativespirits.info/aboriginalculture/law/tribal-punishment-customary-law-payback

67 https://books.google.com.au/books?id=BqBoAgAAQBAJ&pg=PA100&lpg=PA100&dq=payback+for+9/11&source=bl&ots=gfLsZ4rTsH&sig=LldGggmqkhdihb5YRAIpnqS4jE0&hl=en&sa=X&ved=0ahUKEwiQnb6iiozRAhWFEpQKHYEVCis4ChDoAQhaMAk#v=onepage&q=payback%20for%209%2F11&f=false

68 https://en.wikipedia.org/wiki/List_of_genocides_by_death_toll

69 https://www.ushmm.org/confront-genocide/justice-and-accountability/introduction-to-the-definition-of-genocide

70 http://guides.library.jhu.edu/c.php?g=202502&p=1335759

71 College system in the USA or the determining particular electoral borders to balance the voice from the less populated areas. However, the principle remains a majority of the elected members.

72 https://plato.stanford.edu/entries/sorites-paradox/

73 http://w2.vatican.va/content/leo-xiii/en/encyclicals/documents/hf_l-xiii_enc_15051891_rerum-novarum.html

74 https://en.wikipedia.org/wiki/Eugenics

75 Williams, Daniel K., *Defenders of the Unborn*, Oxford University Press 2016

76 http://www.theatlantic.com/politics/archive/2016/02/daniel-williams-defenders-unborn/435369

77 https://en.wikipedia.org/wiki/Roe_v._Wade

78 https://www.scientificamerican.com/article/human-population-reaches-seven-billion

79 https://en.wikipedia.org/wiki/The_Death_of_Socrates

80 http://www.dictionary.com/browse/hara-kiri

81 https://prezi.com/m0fjy_afndad/suicide-in-ancient-rome

82 http://www.usatoday.com/story/news/world/2013/06/13/un-world-pop-

ulation-81-billion-2025/2420989
83 https://en.wikipedia.org/wiki/Age_of_Enlightenment
84 http://www.vaughns-1-pagers.com/history/world-population-growth.htm
85 https://www.verywell.com/longevity-throughout-history-2224054
86 http://www.dailytelegraph.com.au/news/nsw/elderly-dying-with-dignity-sydney-doctors-trial-plan-to-help-patients-decide/news-story/8b0f20b97e300594805f7b1883a68020
87 https://blogs.scientificamerican.com/doing-good-science/who-matters-or-should-when-scientists-engage-in-ethical-decision-making/
88 https://en.wikipedia.org/wiki/Triage
89 https://en.wikipedia.org/wiki/Hippocratic_Oath
90 http://medical-dictionary.thefreedictionary.com/in+vitro+fertilization
91 https://www.theguardian.com/money/2015/oct/13/half-world-wealth-in-hands-population-inequality-report
92 http://www.voicesofyouth.org/en/posts/my-earth--my-responsibility
93 https://en.wikipedia.org/wiki/Anthropology_of_religion
94 http://www.commondreams.org/news/2016/06/20/refugee-planet-there-have-never-been-many-displaced-people-earth

Chapter 4

95 Nigel Nicholson is professor of organisation behaviour at the London Business School. He writes about the 'I" in leadership being a genetic trait. https://www.london.edu/faculty-and-research/lbsr/i-in-leadership#.WGgnhPVOKHs

96 Harvard Business Review https://hbr.org/1998/07/how-hardwired-is-human-behavior

97 Rosenberg, Alexander, *The atheist's guide to reality: enjoying life without illusions*. 1st edition. W.W. Norton 2011

98 https://en.wikipedia.org/wiki/Frans_de_Waal

99 De Waal, Frans, *The Bonobo and the Atheist*, 2013 ISBN 978-0-393-07377-5

100 https://en.wikipedia.org/wiki/Social_anthropology

101 https://en.wikipedia.org/wiki/Charles_Darwin

102 https://en.oxforddictionaries.com/definition/DNA

103 https://www.interpol.int/INTERPOL-expertise/Forensics

104 Grant, Steen, *DNA and Destiny: Nature and Nurture in Human Behavior*, Plenum Press, New York and London, 1996.

105 https://en.wikipedia.org/wiki/Eugenics

106 https://en.wikipedia.org/wiki/Nature_versus_nurture

107 https://en.wikipedia.org/wiki/An_Essay_Concerning_Human_Understanding

108 http://www.iep.utm.edu/descarte

109 https://en.wikipedia.org/wiki/David_Hume

110 https://www.britannica.com/biography/Gottfried-Wilhelm-Leibniz

111 http://www.tabletmag.com/jewish-arts-and-culture/books/122502/our-abraham-not-theirs Levenson, Jon D, *Inheriting Abraham, The legacy of the Patriarch in Judaism, Christianity and Islam*. Princeton University Press. 2012.

112 https://en.wikipedia.org/wiki/Laozi

113 https://en.wikipedia.org/wiki/Confucius

114 http://asiasociety.org/education/origins-buddhism

115 Laozi ; translated and commented by Roberts, Moss, *Dao De Jing: The Book of the Way*, University of California Press, 2004.

116 https://en.wikipedia.org/wiki/DNA

117 https://www.ncbi.nlm.nih.gov/pmc/articles/PMC1893020

118 https://www.uq.edu.au/news/article/2015/05/nature-v-nurture-research-shows-its-both

119 Berger, Peter and Luckmann, Thomas, *The Social Construction of Reality*, Penguin 1966

120 Russell, Bertrand, *On Education*, Routledge, 1926.

121 https://en.wikipedia.org/wiki/Consensus_decision-making

122 https://www.verywell.com/what-is-groupthink-2795213

Chapter 5

123 https://en.wikipedia.org/wiki/It_takes_a_village

124 http://www.lawhandbook.org.au/2016_04_02_03_child_support

125 http://www.abc.net.au/pm/content/2007/s1963979.htm

126 http://reflectd.co/2015/03/19/the-three-most-basic-psychological-needs-and-why-we-need-to-satisfy-them

127 Baumeister, R. F., & Leary, M. R., The need to belong: Desire for interpersonal attachments as a fundamental human motivation. *Psychological Bulletin, 117(3)*, 497-529. 1995.

128 Gagne, Marylene editor, *The Oxford Handbook of Work Engagement, Motivation and Self-determination Theory*, Oxford University Press, 2014.

129 https://www.plimoth.org/sites/default/files/media/pdf/edmaterials_demographics.pdf

130 https://www.compassion.com.au/blog/why-do-the-poor-have-large-

families
131 http://www.who.int/bulletin/volumes/86/3/07-045658/en
132 http://news.nationalgeographic.com/2015/11/151113-datapoints-china-one-child-policy
133 http://blogs.worldbank.org/health/female-education-and-childbearing-closer-look-data
134 https://www.compassion.com.au/blog/why-do-the-poor-have-large-families
135 https://www.thetrumpet.com/article/10541.24
136 Beals. Alan R, *Golapur: A South Indian Village*. Halt, Reinhart and Winston, New York, 1962.
137 Colliver. Philip H, *Jie Marriage* in Cultures and Societies of Africa, edited by Simon and Phoebe Ottenberg, Random House, New York, 1960. pp 190–198.
138 http://www.encyclopedia.com/social-sciences-and-law/anthropology-and-archaeology/customs-and-artifacts/harem
139 https://www.psychologytoday.com/blog/out-the-darkness/201208/why-men-oppress-women
140 https://www.loc.gov/rr/frd/Military_Law/pdf/GC_1949-IV.pdf
141 http://www.bbc.com/news/world-middle-east-30573385
142 http://www.equalitynow.org/traffickingFAQ
143 http://www.ohchr.org/en/professionalinterest/pages/crc.aspx
144 http://www.antislavery.org/english/slavery_today/child_slavery
145 https://www.theguardian.com/society/2016/nov/26/does-britain-take-too-many-children-into-care
146 https://www.childabuseroyalcommission.gov.au
147 https://ourworldindata.org/future-world-population-growth

Chapter 6

148 http://web.mnstate.edu/robertsb/313/petersgolden5e_ch01.pdf
149 http://www.ancient-origins.net/myths-legends/inti-sun-god-inca-spawned-first-rulers-unforgettable-empire-007317
150 http://www.iep.utm.edu/daoism
151 https://en.wikipedia.org/wiki/King_James_Version
152 https://en.wikipedia.org/wiki/King_James_Version
153 https://en.wikipedia.org/wiki/New_International_Version
154 https://en.wikipedia.org/wiki/List_of_Christian_denominations
155 http://www.everystudent.com/features/bible.html

156 http://forward.com/schmooze/338440/when-was-the-bible-really-written-new-clues-emerge
157 https://en.wikipedia.org/wiki/Authorship_of_the_Bible
158 https://www.quora.com/How-can-the-gospels-be-reliable-if-they-were-written-so-long-after-Jesus-died
159 "Mapping the Global Muslim Population: A Report on the Size and Distribution of the World's Muslim Population". Pew Research Center. *October 7, 2009. Retrieved 2013-09-24.* Of the total Muslim population, 10–13% are Shia Muslims and 87–90% are Sunni Muslims.
160 https://en.wikipedia.org/wiki/Muhammad%27s_first_revelation
161 https://en.wikipedia.org/wiki/Hinduism
162 https://en.wikipedia.org/wiki/Jewish_religious_movements
163 https://en.wikipedia.org/wiki/Jewish_religious_movements
164 https://en.wikipedia.org/wiki/The_Church_of_Jesus_Christ_of_Latter-day_Saints
165 https://en.wikipedia.org/wiki/Scientology
166 http://www.un.org/en/udhrbook/pdf/udhr_booklet_en_web.pdf
167 Littman, D. *Universal Human Rights and Human Rights in Islam* (February–March 1999)
168 https://en.wikipedia.org/wiki/Cairo_Declaration_on_Human_Rights_in_Islam
169 https://en.wikipedia.org/wiki/Slavery_in_Africa
170 Wiredu, Kwasi *Towards decolonising African philosophy and religion.* African Studies Quarterly. 1 (4) : 17, 1998. http://asq.africa.ufl.edu/files/Vol-1-Issue-4-Wiredu.pdf
171 Waghid, Jusef *African Philosophy of Education Reconsidered.* Routledge 2014
172 https://en.wikipedia.org/wiki/Divine_right_of_kings
173 https://en.wikipedia.org/wiki/French_Revolution
174 https://en.wikipedia.org/wiki/Russian_Revolution
175 https://en.wikipedia.org/wiki/English_Civil_War
176 https://en.wikipedia.org/wiki/Nicolae_Ceau%C8%99escu
177 https://en.wikipedia.org/wiki/Spread_of_Islam
178 https://en.wikipedia.org/wiki/Islamic_Golden_Age
179 https://en.wikipedia.org/wiki/Crusades
180 de Botton, Alain *Religion for Atheists – A non-believer's guide to the uses of religion.* Penguin, UK, 2012. https://en.wikipedia.org/wiki/Religion_for_Atheists

Chapter 7

181 https://en.wikipedia.org/wiki/Dark_Ages_(historiography)
182 http://news.nationalgeographic.com/news/2011/11/111111-vikings-sunstones-crystals-navigation-science/
183 https://en.wikipedia.org/wiki/The_Dark_Ages:_An_Age_of_Light
184 https://en.wikipedia.org/wiki/Huns
185 https://en.wikipedia.org/wiki/Vandals
186 https://en.wikipedia.org/wiki/Goths
187 https://en.wikipedia.org/wiki/Siege_of_Baghdad_(1258)
188 https://en.wikipedia.org/wiki/Girih
189 https://en.wikipedia.org/wiki/Ibn_Mu%CA%BF%C4%81dh_al-Jayy%C4%81n%C4%AB
190 https://en.wikipedia.org/wiki/Ibn_al-Haytham
191 https://en.wikipedia.org/wiki/Muhammad_ibn_Zakariya_al-Razi
192 https://en.wikipedia.org/wiki/Fatimid_Caliphate
193 https://en.wikipedia.org/wiki/Saladin
194 https://en.wikipedia.org/wiki/Illuminated_manuscript
195 http://islamichistory.org/islamic-golden-age

Chapter 8

196 http://www.independent.co.uk/news/world/politics/oxfam-warns-davos-of-pernicious-impact-of-the-widening-wealth-gap-9070714.html
197 http://www.worldometers.info/world-population/
198 https://publications.credit-suisse.com/tasks/render/file/?fileID=F2425415-DCA7-80B8-EAD989AF9341D47E
199 http://www.msn.com/en-au/money/markets/middle-classes-in-crisis-imfs-christine-lagarde-tells-davos-2017/ar-AAlZ5Sr?li=AAgfYrC&ocid=-mailsignout
200 https://www.theguardian.com/business/2017/jan/18/middle-classes-imf-christine-lagarde-davos-2017-joe-biden
201 http://blogs.artinfo.com/secrethistoryofart/2011/10/24/5-minute-history-of-napoleonic-art-looting
202 http://sam.gov.tr/wp-content/uploads/2012/01/Raymond-Hinnebusch.pdf
203 https://en.wikipedia.org/wiki/The_empire_on_which_the_sun_never_sets
204 http://www.nairaland.com/73798/legendary-harold-smith-speaks-nigeria

205 http://www.denverpost.com/2017/01/16/eight-richest-people/
206 http://www.espnfc.com.au/story/3169463/paris-saint-germain-announce-signing-of-neymar-from-barcelona
207 https://en.wikipedia.org/wiki/Rudd_Concession
208 http://www.telegraph.co.uk/business/2016/07/20/revealed-the-biggest-companies-in-the-world-in-2016/
209 https://en.wikipedia.org/wiki/List_of_countries_by_external_debt
210 http://money.cnn.com/2016/08/30/technology/apple-tax-ruling-numbers/index.html
211 http://www.cnbc.com/2016/11/23/apple-captures-record-91-percent-of-global-smartphone-profits-research.html
212 https://en.wikipedia.org/wiki/Mahabharata

Chapter 9

213 Piketty, Thomas, *Capital in the 21st Century*, Harvard University Press, 2014.
214 http://www.inc-cap.com/
215 https://www.theguardian.com/environment/earth-insight/2014/may/28/inclusive-capitalism-trojan-horse-global-revolt-henry-jackson-society-pr-growth
216 http://evatt.org.au/papers/inclusive-capitalism.html
217 https://en.wikipedia.org/wiki/Three-card_Monte
218 Stiglitz, J, *The Price of Inequality: How today's divided society endangers our future*. W.W.Norton, New York, 2012.
219 https://www.weforum.org/agenda/2016/07/it-s-time-to-demolish-the-myth-of-trickle-down-economics/
220 https://en.wikipedia.org/wiki/Matthew_effect
221 https://en.wikipedia.org/wiki/Opium_of_the_people
222 https://en.wikipedia.org/wiki/Grand_Tour
223 https://en.wikipedia.org/wiki/Noblesse_oblige
224 https://en.wikipedia.org/wiki/Andrew_Carnegie
225 https://en.wikipedia.org/wiki/The_Gospel_of_Wealth
226 Rhodes, Cecil. Stead, William Thomas, ed. *The Last Will and Testament of Cecil John Rhodes*, with Elucidatory Notes, to which are Added Some Chapters Describing the Political and Religious Ideas of the Testator. *London. 1902.*
227 https://en.wikipedia.org/wiki/Philanthropy_in_the_United_States
228 https://en.wikipedia.org/wiki/Benjamin_Franklin
229 http://www.abrahamlincolnonline.org/lincoln/speeches/gettysburg.htm
230 https://en.wikipedia.org/wiki/Mark_Zuckerberg

231 https://en.wikipedia.org/wiki/Bill_Gates
232 https://en.wikipedia.org/wiki/Warren_Buffett
233 https://en.wikipedia.org/wiki/Warren_Buffett
234 Frank, Robert. *The Rich Are Less Charitable Than the Middle Class: Study.* CNBC. 2012 Retrieved February 21, 2014
235 https://en.wikipedia.org/wiki/The_Chronicle_of_Philanthropy
236 http://www.globalethicsuniversity.com/articles/greed.htm
237 https://en.wikipedia.org/wiki/Richard_G._Wilkinson
238 https://en.wikipedia.org/wiki/TED_(conference)
https://www.ted.com/talks/richard_wilkinson/transcript?language=en
239 http://inequality.org/richard-wilkinson-economic-inequality-harms-societies/ Wilkinson, R and Pickett, K. *The Spirit Level: Why greater equality makes societies stronger,* Bloomsbury, New York, 2011.
240 https://inequalitiesblog.wordpress.com/2010/09/29/wilkinson-pickett-are-they-right/
241 https://en.wikipedia.org/wiki/Red_herring
242 https://www.one.org/international/blog/inspiration-mandelas-speech-in-trafalgar-square/

Chapter 10

243 http://www.truthdig.com/report/item/we_need_a_new_economic_model_because_current_model_falling_apart_20150318
244 http://insights.som.yale.edu/insights/what-is-ecological-economics
https://crawford.anu.edu.au/news-events/news/226/planting-seeds-new-world-economy
https://crawford.anu.edu.au/sites/default/files/news/files/2013-04/anu_foundation_lecture_2013.pdf
245 http://fuelfix.com/blog/2016/07/14/bp-estimates-cost-of-2010-gulf-oil-spill-at-61-6-billion/
246 http://business.time.com/2012/05/28/why-companies-can-no-longer-afford-to-ignore-their-social-responsibilities
247 https://en.wikipedia.org/wiki/Genuine_progress_indicator
248 http://www.independent.co.uk/news/world/europe/refugee-crisis-migrants-world-day-un-a7090986.html
249 https://en.wikipedia.org/wiki/Silent_Spring
250 https://en.wikipedia.org/wiki/The_Population_Bomb
251 http://www.urbandictionary.com/define.php?term=same%20old%2C%20same%20old
252 https://en.wikipedia.org/wiki/Trickle-down_economics

253 https://www.britannica.com/topic/Financial-Crisis-of-2008-The-1484264

254 http://www.dailymail.co.uk/news/article-1248648/MP-expenses-Shaming-389-greedy-politicians-went-far.html

255 http://www.theaustralian.com.au/news/inquirer/travel-rorts-mps-who-have-paid-the-price/news-story/ca95f63e05b6629f1c5398b582a9636b

256 https://en.wikipedia.org/wiki/Karl_Marx

257 https://en.wikipedia.org/wiki/McCarthyism

258 https://en.wikipedia.org/wiki/Cold_War

259 https://en.wikipedia.org/wiki/Joseph_Stalin

260 https://en.wikipedia.org/wiki/Gulag

261 https://en.wikipedia.org/wiki/Berlin_Wall

262 https://en.wikipedia.org/wiki/Negotiations_to_end_apartheid_in_South_Africa

263 http://businessresearcher.sagepub.com/sbr-1645-94858-2644624/20150202/flat-management

264 https://en.wikipedia.org/wiki/Poverty_in_China

265 https://en.wikipedia.org/wiki/My_Lai_Massacre

266 http://www.abc.net.au/news/2015-12-09/harrison-ford-hits-out-at-global-inaction-on-climate-change/7015380

267 https://news.mongabay.com/2013/10/david-attenborough-someone-who-believes-in-infinite-growth-is-either-a-madman-or-an-economist

268 http://www.bbc.com/news/uk-14432401

269 http://nsidc.org/greenland-today

270 https://en.wikipedia.org/wiki/Renewable_energy_debate

271 http://knowledge.wharton.upenn.edu/article/behind-the-curve-have-us-automakers-built-the-wrong-cars-at-the-wrong-time-again

272 http://www.keating.org.au/shop/item/human-resource-management-the-role-of-leadership-11-may-2004

273 https://en.wikipedia.org/wiki/Law_of_the_instrument

274 http://www.telospress.com/iris-murdoch-on-virtue

Chapter 11

275 Caramazza, A. *Scientific American Mind* 20, 11. 2010 http://www.readcube.com/articles/10.1038/scientificamericanmind0110-11

For those with a medical science inclination: https://academic.oup.com/brain/article/138/6/1679/2847628/Functional-connectivity-of-visual-cortex-in-the

276 https://www.scientificamerican.com/article/wired-for-categorization

277 https://opentextbc.ca/introductiontosociology/chapter/chapter5-socialization

278 https://en.wikipedia.org/wiki/Myers%E2%80%93Briggs_Type_Indicator#Differences_from_Jung

279 https://en.wikipedia.org/wiki/Emotional_intelligence

280 https://thewisesloth.com/2012/09/02/15-signs-your-church-is-a-cult

Chapter 12

281 http://www.un.org/en/universal-declaration-human-rights

282 https://en.wikipedia.org/wiki/Cairo_Declaration_on_Human_Rights_in_Islam

283 https://en.wikipedia.org/wiki/Queen_Victoria

284 Jawad, Haifaa A. *The Rights of Women in Islam: An Authentic Approach.* Palgrave Macmillan. 1998. p20. ISBN 978-0333734582

285 https://en.wikipedia.org/wiki/Muslim_female_political_leaders

286 Eaton, Gai *Remembering God: Reflections on Islam.* Cambridge, England: The Islamic Texts Society. 2000. p.93. ISBN 978-0-946621-84-2.

287 Investing in the Children of the Islamic World UNICEF (2007)

288 Adult and Youth Literacy, 1990–2015, UNESCO (2012), ISBN 978-92-9189-117-7

289 Amani Hamdan, *Women and education in Saudi Arabia: Challenges and achievements*, International Education Journal, 6(1), 2005 pp. 42-64

290 http://data.unicef.org/topic/education/literacy

291 http://www.huffingtonpost.com/2013/09/06/illiteracy-rate_n_3880355.html

292 http://www.statisticbrain.com/number-of-american-adults-who-cant-read/

293 http://news.bbc.co.uk/2/shared/spl/hi/uk/06/prisons/html/nn2page1.stm

294 http://www.prisonstudies.org/highest-to-lowest/prison-population-total?field_region_taxonomy_tid=All&=Apply

295 https://en.wikipedia.org/wiki/Charles_I_of_England

296 https://en.wikipedia.org/wiki/Magna_Carta

297 https://en.wikipedia.org/wiki/American_Revolutionary_War

298 https://en.wikipedia.org/wiki/American_Civil_War

299 http://www.newworldencyclopedia.org/entry/French_Revolution

300 https://en.wikipedia.org/wiki/Russian_Revolution

301 http://latinamericanhistory.about.com/od/theconquestofperu/p/Manco-Inca-S-Rebellion-1535-1544.htm

302 http://www.findmypast.com.au/articles/world-records/full-list-of-united-kingdom-records/armed-forces-and-conflict/british-casualties-indian-mutiny-1857-1859

303 https://en.wikipedia.org/wiki/Indian_Rebellion_of_1857

304 http://metro.co.uk/2017/02/13/assads-holocaust-corpses-lined-up-show-scale-of-atrocities-6444710

Chapter 13

305 http://dictionary.cambridge.org/dictionary/english/tabloid

306 https://en.wikipedia.org/wiki/Confirmation_bias

307 https://en.wikipedia.org/wiki/Fact

308 http://www.todayifoundout.com/index.php/2010/02/the-difference-between-a-fact-and-a-factoid

309 https://en.wikipedia.org/wiki/Availability_heuristic

310 https://en.wikipedia.org/wiki/Fallacy

311 http://www.independent.co.uk/news/world/americas/hillary-clinton-fake-news-conspiracy-theory-child-sex-ring-edgar-maddison-welch-open-fire-comet-ping-a7456021.html

312 https://www.theguardian.com/us-news/2017/jan/22/donald-trump-kellyanne-conway-inauguration-alternative-facts

313 https://www.theguardian.com/us-news/2017/feb/28/full-transcript-donald-trump-presidential-address-congress

314 https://www.nytimes.com/2017/02/13/opinion/why-saying-radical-islamic-terrorism-isnt-enough.html

315 https://en.wikipedia.org/wiki/Executive_Order_13769

316 https://en.wikipedia.org/wiki/David_Neiwert

317 https://en.wikipedia.org/wiki/Center_for_Investigative_Reporting

318 https://www.revealnews.org/article/home-is-where-the-hate-is/

319 https://en.wikipedia.org/wiki/List_of_fallacies

320 https://en.wikipedia.org/wiki/Sorites_paradox

321 http://www.bioethics.org.uk/evidenceguide.html

322 https://en.wikipedia.org/wiki/Jeanne_Calment

323 http://www.forbes.com/sites/stratfor/2017/02/02/alternative-facts-in-a-post-truth-world/#3501cc576d60

324 https://www.theguardian.com/media/greenslade/2016/aug/25/why-media-commentary-is-so-crucial-when-op

325 https://en.wikipedia.org/wiki/C._P._Scott

326 https://en.wikipedia.org/wiki/David_Lloyd_George

327 https://en.wikipedia.org/wiki/Leveson_Inquiry

328 https://www.washingtonpost.com/news/the-fix/wp/2017/02/25/the-remarkable-inconsistency-of-trumps-attacks-on-the-media/?utm_term=.4ec401b8ab4d

329 http://www.mintpressnews.com/pants-on-fire-analysis-shows-60-of-fox-news-facts-are-really-lies/205563

330 http://www.esquire.com/news-politics/politics/news/a53269/trump-florida-rally-lies

331 http://theconversation.com/hard-evidence-analysis-shows-extent-of-press-bias-towards-brexit-61106

332 http://www.abc.net.au/4corners/stories/2017/04/10/4649443.htm

333 http://quoteinvestigator.com/2013/04/23/good-idea

Chapter 14

334 https://en.wikipedia.org/wiki/Albert_Einstein

335 https://en.wikipedia.org/wiki/Newton%27s_law_of_universal_gravitation

336 https://en.wikipedia.org/wiki/Theory_of_relativity#Development_and_acceptance

337 http://www.npr.org/2017/02/17/515630467/with-fake-news-trump-moves-from-alternative-facts-to-alternative-language

338 https://en.wikipedia.org/wiki/Availability_heuristic

339 An oft quoted Biblical reference https://www.openbible.info/topics/practice_what_you_preach

340 Russell, Bertrand, *On Education*, Routledge, 1926.

341 https://en.wikipedia.org/wiki/Usain_Bolt

342 https://en.wikipedia.org/wiki/Leonardo_da_Vinci

343 http://www.ushistory.org/DECLARATION/document

344 https://en.wikipedia.org/wiki/Anti-miscegenation_laws_in_the_United_States

345 https://en.wikipedia.org/wiki/Christianity_and_colonialism

346 http://www.saburchill.com/history/chapters/IR/039a.html

347 https://en.wikipedia.org/wiki/Ku_Klux_Klan

348 https://en.wikipedia.org/wiki/The_Clansman:_A_Historical_Romance_of_the_Ku_Klux_Klan

349 https://en.wikipedia.org/wiki/The_Birth_of_a_Nation

350 https://en.wikipedia.org/wiki/Islamic_State_of_Iraq_and_the_Levant

351 http://www.independent.co.uk/news/world/middle-east/isis-sex-slaves-lamiya-aji-bashar-nadia-murad-sinjar-yazidi-genocide-sexual-violence-rape-sakharov-a7445151.html

352 https://en.wikipedia.org/wiki/White_Australia_policy

353 Holt, Albert, *Murri on a Mission: Gunnan Gunnan*. The Rams Skull Press, Queensland. 2014. ISBN 9781875872879 and https://www.bookdepository.com/Forcibly-Removed-Albert-Holt/9781875641642

354 https://en.wikipedia.org/wiki/European_Australians

355 https://en.wikipedia.org/wiki/Kanaka_(Pacific_Island_worker)

356 https://en.wikipedia.org/wiki/Post-war_immigration_to_Australia

357 http://closingthegap.pmc.gov.au/sites/default/files/ctg-report-2017.pdf

358 https://en.wikipedia.org/wiki/History_of_eugenics

359 https://en.wikipedia.org/wiki/On_the_Origin_of_Species

360 https://en.wikipedia.org/wiki/Infanticide#Greece_and_Rome

361 https://www.psychologytoday.com/blog/feeling-too-much/201408/islands-genius-how-savants-do-what-they-do

362 http://spartareconsidered.blogspot.com.au/2011/11/infanticide-in-sparta-and-athens.html

363 http://www.dailymail.co.uk/health/article-2462640/Five-million-babies-born-IVF--HALF-2007.html

364 de Waal, Frans. "Our Inner Ape: A Leading Primatologist Explains Why We Are Who We Are". 1997 Science Shelf. Retrieved 2013-11-21.

Chapter 15

365 http://www.greenland.com/en/about-greenland/culture-spirit/history/myths-and-legends/the-inuits-view-of-life

366 https://whitleyaward.org/winners/mapping-traditional-fishing-marine-protected-areas-punta-san-juan-peru

367 http://www.scottmanning.com/content/growing-up-spartan

368 http://www.ohchr.org/EN/ProfessionalInterest/Pages/CRC.aspx

369 http://euthanasia.procon.org/view.resource.php?resourceID=000126

370 https://en.wikipedia.org/wiki/Garrett_Hardin

371 http://hmontenegrotok.blogspot.com.au/2015/04/the-lifeboat-dilemma.html

372 http://library.uniteddiversity.coop/More_Books_and_Reports/Silent_Spring-Rachel_Carson-1962.pdf

373 http://www.geo.mtu.edu/~asmayer/rural_sustain/governance/Hardin%201968.pdf

374 http://www.uvm.edu/~gflomenh/ENV-NGO-PA395/articles/Lynn-White.pdf

375 https://en.wikipedia.org/wiki/A_Sand_County_Almanac

376 https://www.theguardian.com/environment/2015/dec/13/paris-climate-deal-cop-diplomacy-developing-united-nations

377 https://en.wikipedia.org/wiki/List_of_G20_summits

378 https://en.wikipedia.org/wiki/John_Dalberg-Acton,_1st_Baron_Acton
https://history.hanover.edu/courses/excerpts/165acton.html

379 http://history.hanover.edu/courses/excerpts/165acton.html

380 https://www.seeker.com/how-dictators-keep-control-discovery-news-1765571212.html

381 https://en.wikipedia.org/wiki/Ubuntu_(philosophy)

382 http://onlinelibrary.wiley.com/doi/10.1111/j.1469-5812.2011.00792.x/abstract
http://onlinelibrary.wiley.com/doi/10.1111/epat.2012.44.issue-s2/issuetoc

383 https://www.washingtonpost.com/local/nelson-mandela-a-colossus-of-unimpeachable-moral-character/2013/12/06/0a2cd28a-5ec9-11e3-be07-006c776266ed_story.html?utm_term=.bddbb0fa0d85
file:///C:/Users/User/Downloads/religions-03-00369.pdf

384 https://en.wikipedia.org/wiki/Truth_and_Reconciliation_Commission_(South_Africa)

385 https://simple.wikipedia.org/wiki/Apartheid_in_South_Africa

386 https://en.wikipedia.org/wiki/Nuremberg_trials

387 https://www.theguardian.com/world/2016/jun/17/auschwitz-guard-reinhold-hanning-jailed-holocaust-auschwitz

388 https://www.trumanlibrary.org/executiveorders/index.php?pid=629&st=&st1=
https://books.google.com.au/books?id=ojjEDQAAQBAJ&pg=PA356&lpg=PA356&dq=executive+order+10393+1954&source=bl&ots=GrRss3wigE&sig=U6pZILRDzcDkKCfA72BvcmF4zw8&hl=en&sa=X&ved=0ahUKEwj5ktah2PrSAhULerwKHQvRASoQ6AEIMTAE#v=onepage&q=executive%20order%2010393%201954&f=false

389 https://en.wikipedia.org/wiki/International_Military_Tribunal_for_the_Far_East

390 http://warfarehistorynetwork.com/daily/wwii/macarthurs-occupation-of-japan-lessons-of-counterinsurgency

391 https://qz.com/93070/the-wisdom-of-mandela-quotes-from-the-most-inspiring-leader-of-the-20th-century/

392 https://en.wikipedia.org/wiki/One_Day_in_the_Life_of_Ivan_Denisovich

Chapter 16

393 https://en.wikipedia.org/wiki/Benjamin_Libet

394 https://prezi.com/_bpsguy7olr7/wegner-wheatley-1999-apparent-mental-causation

395 https://blogs.scientificamerican.com/mind-guest-blog/what-neuroscience-says-about-free-will

396 http://www.independent.co.uk/news/science/free-will-could-all-be-an-illusion-scientists-suggest-after-study-that-shows-choice-could-just-be-a7008181.html

397 https://en.wikipedia.org/wiki/Alexander_Rosenberg

398 https://en.wikipedia.org/wiki/Scientism

399 http://blog.talkingphilosophy.com/?p=4209

400 *Islām.* Encyclopædia Britannica *Online.* Encyclopædia Britannica *Inc. The Arabic term islām, literally 'surrender', illuminates the fundamental religious idea of Islam — that the believer (called a Muslim, from the active particle of islām) accepts surrender to the will of Allah (in Arabic, Allāh: God).*

401 https://www.thoughtco.com/karl-marx-on-religion-251019

402 The Stanford Prison Experiment: A Simulation Study of the Psychology of Imprisonment. Web. 1 Apr. 2011". *Prisonexp.org.* Retrieved 2013-05-21.

403 https://en.wikipedia.org/wiki/Free_will

404 https://en.wikipedia.org/wiki/Martin_Seligman

405 https://en.wikipedia.org/wiki/Mens_rea

406 http://users.tpg.com.au/raeda/website/guilty.htm

407 http://farragut.bownet.org/draynard/DoWeHaveFreeWillarticle.pdf

408 http://www.creativitypost.com/science/has_neuro_science_buried_free_will

409 Dennett, Daniel. *Elbow Room: The Varieties of Free Will Worth Wanting.* MIT Press, Cambridge, Massachusetts. 1984.

410 https://en.wikipedia.org/wiki/Elbow_Room_(book)

411 http://bigthink.com/videos/daniel-dennett-explains-consciousness-and-free-will

412 Dennett, Daniel. (1992) *Consciousness Explained*, Back Bay Books 1992 (ISBN 0-316-18066-1) Further reading: http://open-mind.net/collection.pdf

413 https://en.wikipedia.org/wiki/Daniel_Dennett

414 https://www.youtube.com/watch?v=KeCByjosT4U

415 https://en.wikipedia.org/wiki/Sam_Harris

416 Harris, Sam *Free Will*, 2012. ISBN 978145168340 https://en.wikipedia.org/wiki/Free_Will

417 https://en.wikipedia.org/wiki/Sam_Harris

Chapter 17

418 https://en.wikipedia.org/wiki/Gettysburg_Address
419 https://en.wikipedia.org/wiki/Athenian_democracy
420 https://simple.wikipedia.org/wiki/Constitutional_republic
421 https://en.wikipedia.org/wiki/Constitutional_monarchy
422 https://en.wikipedia.org/wiki/Gerrymandering
423 https://en.wikipedia.org/wiki/Gerrymandering_in_the_United_States
424 http://www.irishtimes.com/news/politics/how-do-minority-governments-work-in-europe-and-elsewhere-1.2628415
425 https://en.wikipedia.org/wiki/Whip_(politics)
426 http://www.smh.com.au/federal-politics/political-news/time-stands-still-in-parliament-house-as-a-filibustering-senate-holds-itself-hostage-20170330-gval3h.html
427 https://en.wikipedia.org/wiki/Filibuster
428 http://www.urbandictionary.com/define.php?term=Political%20Speak
429 https://en.wikipedia.org/wiki/Doublespeak
430 https://en.wikipedia.org/wiki/Social_media_and_the_Arab_Spring
431 https://richardlangworth.com/worst-form-of-government

Chapter 18

432 http://www.winstonchurchill.org/resources/quotations/the-worst-form-of-government
433 https://www.boundless.com/political-science/textbooks/boundless-political-science-textbook/american-politics-1/forms-of-government-19/non-democratic-governments-monarchy-oligarchy-technocracy-and-theocracy-116-10688
434 https://en.wikipedia.org/wiki/Ideology
435 https://en.wikipedia.org/wiki/Capitalism
436 http://www.worldsocialism.org/english/what-capitalism
437 https://en.wikipedia.org/wiki/Economic_growth
438 https://en.wikipedia.org/wiki/The_Communist_Manifesto
439 https://simple.wikipedia.org/wiki/Communism
440 https://en.wikipedia.org/wiki/Joseph_Stalin
441 http://www.businessinsider.com/how-china-went-from-communist-to-capitalist-2015-
442 https://en.wikipedia.org/wiki/Army%E2%80%93McCarthy_hearings
443 Boundless. *"Non-Democratic Governments: Monarchy, Oligarchy, Technocracy, and Theocracy." Boundless Political Science* Boundless, 26 May 2004.

444 https://en.wikipedia.org/wiki/Murray_Bookchin

445 https://en.wikipedia.org/wiki/Communalism_(political_philosophy)

446 Gyekye, K. *Person and community in Akan thought*. In: Wiredu, K. & Gyekye, K. (Eds.), Person and Community (Washington: The Council for Research in Values and Philosophy), 101–122, 1992.

447 https://en.wikipedia.org/wiki/Smoke_and_mirrors

448 http://www.thedailybeast.com/articles/2014/11/08/is-it-time-to-take-a-chance-on-random-representatives.html

449 http://www.abc.net.au/news/2011-03-18/random-selection-could-improve-democracy/2653044

450 https://en.wikipedia.org/wiki/Reserved_political_positions

451 https://en.wikipedia.org/wiki/Tasmanian_House_of_Assembly

452 https://en.wikipedia.org/wiki/Single_transferable_vote

453 https://sweden.se/society/gender-equality-in-sweden/

454 https://en.wikipedia.org/wiki/Women_in_the_42nd_Canadian_Parliament

455 http://www.aph.gov.au/About_Parliament/Parliamentary_Departments/Parliamentary_Library/FlagPost/2016/August/The_gender_composition_of_the_45th_parliament

456 http://democracyinafrica.org/gender-quotas-womens-representation-african-parliaments/

Chapter 19

457 http://www.infoplease.com/ipa/A0762181.html

458 https://ourworldindata.org/terrorism/

459 http://www.abs.gov.au/census

460 http://www.news.com.au/national/no-religion-tops-religion-question-in-census/news-story/a3b45e6b2e35df695932a83535078f51

461 http://www.abs.gov.au/AUSSTATS/abs@.nsf/mediareleasesbyReleaseDate/7E65A144540551D7CA258148000E2B85?OpenDocument

462 http://www.start.umd.edu/gtd/

463 https://ourworldindata.org/terrorism/

464 https://en.wikipedia.org/wiki/Fallacy_of_composition

465 https://en.wikipedia.org/wiki/Canon_law

466 http://www.alrc.gov.au/publications/21.%20Aboriginal%20Customary%20Laws%20and%20Sentencing/aboriginal-customary-laws-and-notion-%E2%80%98puni

467 http://www.news.com.au/entertainment/tv/this-is-what-sharia-law-actually-is/news-story/bc87221d32afe4fa4013a07b38fda32e

https://en.wikipedia.org/wiki/Sharia

468 http://dwindlinginunbelief.blogspot.com.au/2006/09/death-by-stoning-bible-vs-quran.html

469 http://www.news.com.au/entertainment/tv/this-is-what-sharia-law-actually-is/news-story/bc87221d32afe4fa4013a07b38fda32e

470 https://www.theguardian.com/commentisfree/2015/mar/16/moderate-muslim-devout-liberal-religion

471 http://www.dailylife.com.au/news-and-views/dl-culture/i-follow-shari-ah-this-is-what-it-really-means-to-me-20160707-gq143i.html

472 http://www.abc.net.au/news/2017-02-25/mem-fox-detained-at-los-angeles-airport-by-us-officials/8303366

473 https://en.wikipedia.org/wiki/Convention_Relating_to_the_Status_of_Refugees

474 https://en.wikipedia.org/wiki/Garrett_Hardin

475 http://www.huffingtonpost.ca/2017/02/20/canada-syrian-refugees_n_14887314.html

476 http://www.aph.gov.au/About_Parliament/Parliamentary_Departments/Parliamentary_Library/pubs/rp/rp1617/RefugeeResettlement#_Toc461022111

https://www.voanews.com/a/indonesia-breaks-silence-on-refugees-with-presidential-decree/3696079.html

477 http://www.unhcr.org/en-au/news/latest/2017/2/58b001ab4/poorer-countries-host-forcibly-displaced-report-shows.html

478 http://www.abc.net.au/news/2016-09-21/where-does-australia-rank-on-its-refugee-intake/7864070

Chapter 20

479 https://hbr.org/2012/01/avoid-the-traps-that-can-destroy-family-businesses

http://www.imd.org/uupload/IMD.WebSite/MicroSites/family-business/pdfs/Family%20Businesses%20%20Successes%20and%20Failures.pdf

480 https://www.slatergordon.com.au/blog/unattended-children-getting-facts-straight

http://www.couriermail.com.au/news/queensland/do-your-kids-walk-or-ride-to-school-by-themselves-you-could-be-breaking-the-law/news-story/d45f1daefac034cb0a7aef961285c88b

http://raisingchildren.net.au/articles/leaving_children_home_alone.html

481 http://www.goldcoastbulletin.com.au/news/gold-coast/wrapping-kids-in-cotton-wool-depriving-them-of-vital-life-experiences/news-story/2a6245655494ba7e830f83ce7ebb4c4b

482 http://www.parents.com/parenting/better-parenting/what-is-helicopter-parenting

483 http://www.themercury.com.au/lifestyle/in-focus-stress-less/news-story/af6c4cc5aaaae7d5761953d65626661d

484 https://www.wanderlustworker.com/12-famous-people-who-failed-before-succeeding

485 http://www.smh.com.au/comment/the-way-we-teach-our-children-is-truly-crazy-20170223-gujyh1.html

486 http://www.telegraph.co.uk/education/10439196/Children-of-rich-parents-suffering-increased-mental-health-problems.html

487 http://www.vulture.com/2014/08/robin-williams-tribute-obituary.html

488 http://www.progressio.org.uk/blog/empowered-blog/nicaragua-%E2%80%98lost-generation%E2%80%99-glue-sniffing-street-children-masaya

489 Read John O'Brien's classic Australian poem 'We'll all be rooned, said Hanrahan' https://en.wikipedia.org/wiki/Said_Hanrahan

490 https://www.theatlantic.com/education/archive/2014/04/the-myth-of-working-your-way-through-college/359735

491 http://university.which.co.uk/advice/career-prospects/getting-a-graduate-job-degree-internship-myths-realities

492 https://en.wikipedia.org/wiki/Siren_(mythology)

493 http://www.slate.com/blogs/the_vault/2015/10/02/how_the_nazis_confiscated_jewish_belongings.html

494 https://www.ushmm.org/wlc/en/article.php?ModuleId=10005687

495 http://blogs.wsj.com/economics/2012/10/01/total-global-losses-from-financial-crisis-15-trillion

496 https://en.wikipedia.org/wiki/Ponzi_scheme

497 http://www.rba.gov.au/speeches/2009/sp-so-150409.html

498 https://en.wikipedia.org/wiki/Homelessness_in_the_United_States

499 http://www.homelessnessaustralia.org.au

500 https://en.wikipedia.org/wiki/Homelessness_in_Canada

501 https://en.wikipedia.org/wiki/2016%E2%80%9317_Rohingya_persecution_in_Myanmar

502 https://en.wikipedia.org/wiki/Yazidis

503 http://www.reuters.com/article/us-southsudan-refugees-kenya-idUSKBN0P00TJ20150620

504 https://en.wikipedia.org/wiki/Lebensraum
505 https://en.wikipedia.org/wiki/Greater_East_Asia_Co-Prosperity_Sphere
506 http://sageamericanhistory.net/worldwar2/docs/Macarthurtokyo.html

Chapter 21

507 Read *Roller Coaster* by Jim Reay 2016. ISBN 9781875872930 Available on Amazon, print on demand

508 https://en.wikipedia.org/wiki/United_Nations_Security_Council_veto_power

509 http://thenode.biologists.com/wp-content/uploads/2013/12/Outreach-activity-DNA-extraction-from-kiwi-fruit.pdf

510 https://www.youtube.com/watch?v=dD9dGFrFcoo
https://www.youtube.com/watch?v=q87D2rqtAc4

511 http://www.andersen.sdu.dk/vaerk/hersholt/theEmperorsNewClothes_e.html
http://www.urbandictionary.com/define.php?term=the%20emporer%20has%20no%20clothes

512 https://en.wikipedia.org/wiki/Jock_Tamson%27s_Bairns

513 https://en.wikipedia.org/wiki/John_Maxwell_Edmonds

514 https://www.poets.org/poetsorg/poem/calf-path

515 http://www.huffingtonpost.com/kicker/is-facebook-controlling-t_b_9959890.html

516 https://www.modernghana.com/music/7892/3/sean-connery-recalls-first-big-break.html

517 Popper, Karl. *The Logic of Scientific Discovery*, Routledge, 1934. Reprinted 2002 https://en.wikiquote.org/wiki/Karl_Popper

518 https://en.wikipedia.org/wiki/Normandy_landings

519 *Newton, Isaac. "Letter from Sir Isaac Newton to Robert Hooke". Historical Society of Pennsylvania. Retrieved 7 August 2016.*

Forgiveness means letting go of the hope for a better past
Lama Surya Das

www.ingramcontent.com/pod-product-compliance
Lightning Source LLC
Chambersburg PA
CBHW051045160426
43193CB00010B/1067